Urban Planning in the 1960s

Marshall Kaplan

Urban Planning
in the 1960s
A Design
for Irrelevancy

The MIT Press
Cambridge, Massachusetts, and London, England

MIT Press

0262610183

KAPLAN
URBAN PLANNING

Original edition copyright © 1973 by Praeger Publishers, Inc., New York

First MIT Press paperback edition, March 1974

Printed in the United States of America

Library of Congress Cataloging in Publication Data

Kaplan, Marshall.
  Urban planning in the 1960s

  Includes bibliographical references.
  1. Cities and towns — Planning — United States. 2. Cities and towns —
Planning — 1945. I. Title. HT167.K33 1974   309.2'62'0973   73-22129
ISBN 0-262-61018-3

As did so many of my colleagues, I began my professional career as an "urbanist" in the late 1950s. Through a combination of luck and some skill, I have been able to respond, seemingly successfully, to a range of different and often challenging assignments given me by varied private and community groups. Along the way I have picked up my share of honorific titles; joined a reasonable number of professional planning organizations; delivered what seems to be in retrospect an abnormally large number of speeches at planning conferences; and for better or worse, written a number of papers and books concerned with urban problems. I state these credits here, not to impress, but to provide a reference point for the critical observations that appear in this book concerning the role of the planning profession.

Indeed, even at the outset it can be said that one need not look far for evidence, even if anecdotal, to show that the impact of the planning profession on the quality of urban life has been marginal at best and, at times, negative. Certainly, twenty years of federal planning assistance programs have not visibly built up the planning capacity of local governments or improved the quality of local life. Indeed, the prime beneficiaries of such aid seem to be, not local governments or local residents, but local and national consultants.

Most plans prepared by most city planners have failed to pay heed to the many culturally and economically determined differences in life style of residents of the nation's cities and suburban areas. Plans, when heeded, have often either led to an allocation of scarce resources away from the least advantaged members of urban society or, as in urban renewal, had a directly negative effect on their lives. Somewhat surprisingly, even the more affluent members of society have not found their legitimate needs and their observed behavior patterns reflected in most community plans.

Planners leaving the local scene for Washington have not fared appreciably better. Many have participated in the development of policies and proposals to reform federal institutions. Consequently, their reports have proposed basic structural reforms and a "coordinated" federal response to urban problems. Not reflecting the basic pluralism inherent in both the political and the institutional facts of life, their reports have had little or no impact. Other planners, not so involved in government efforts at basic reform, have been asked at times to draft planning criteria for local governments to meet prior to receipt of federal aid. Their work has generally resulted in planning models based on a rationale, more appropriate to the college classroom than to cities and towns facing complex political, social, economic, and environmental problems.

It is not easy to pinpoint the reasons for the impotence of the planning profession. I, for one, am convinced, however, that a good part of the blame rests on the unwillingness of planners—and indeed of clients and constituents—to challenge ideas in common currency concerning professional goals, patterns of behavior, and techniques. In this regard, I am convinced, as the articles in this book will show, that for too many years most planners have incorrectly assumed that their commitment to the liberal political tradition required uncritical acceptance of rationalism as a point of departure. Partly for this reason, unproven approaches and such phrases as "long-range planning" and "interdisciplinary analysis" have been uncritically elevated to the position of prescriptions for professional behavior. In the process the planners clear responsibility to link his and other value sets to professional tasks has often been abdicated. Similarly, in the process, the fiction has been widely maintained that his work was above politics and that his professional credentials were somehow superior to those of elected officials or "politically" appointed administrators.

It should be clear by now that I am not satisfied either with the way my profession has developed or with the direction it seems to be taking. I should like to see David Riesman's somewhat premature comments concerning the planner come true; that is, I wish planners could begin to "become reasonably weary of cultural definitions that are systematically trotted out to rationalize the inadequacies of city life today, for the well to do as well as for the poor."* Only if they do so will they be able to contribute to a much-needed national reappraisal of the role of professional planners in future efforts to solve urban problems—a reappraisal that should involve government officials at all levels as well as community and private groups.

I have prepared this volume in the hope that it will contribute to the needed national dialogue concerning the role and impact of the planner in developing relevant national as well as local urban policies and programs. It contains many of the articles I have written over the past dozen years. Selection of each was premised on two primary objectives—first, my desire to offer a consistent and relevant critique of the planning profession and, second, my interest in proposing to

---

*David Riesman, The Lonely Crowd (New York: Doubleday, 1953), p. 348.

the planner, his clients, and his constituents, several relevant alternatives to current approaches.

I have included several papers and articles that offer commentary on current national urban policies and programs. Not to do so would have denied the fact that for the most part national policies and programs provide the context and the environment within which professional planners work. Such an omission would also have weakened my plea that planners relieve themselves of their positivist tendencies and, in effect, become relevant.

ACKNOWLEDGMENTS

It is difficult in this brief space to acknowledge all the individuals who, through friendship and criticism, have helped me grow over the past dozen years as a professional and human being. I must mention a few, however. The late Charles Abrams, national housing and urban expert, provided me, and will continue to provide me, a model to emulate. His superior intellect and love of human beings will be remembered by all whose lives he touched. Fred Adams and Jack Howard of MIT's Planning School gave me and numerous other students the will and desire to engage in self-criticism. Mel Webber, Jack Dyckman, William Wheaton, Bernard Frieden, Harry Spehct, Edward P. Eichler, and Melvin Mogulof have, through their friendship, writings, and comments over the years stimulated some of my thinking concerning the role planners have played in the past and should play in the future.

I also include in this list two of the most thoughtful planners I know—my partners and friends, Sheldon Gans and Howard Kahn. Finally, because without their patience and understanding, my own experiences would have been severely limited and none of the articles included in this book could have been written, I acknowledge the debt I owe to my parents and family—particularly to my wife, Barbara, and my children, Scott and Stevie.

CONTENTS

Chapter   Page

THE PLANNING PROFESSION:
DESIGN FOR IRRELEVANCY

Each of the five chapters included in Part I offers commentary on the state of the planning profession during the 1960s. Each also provides a consistent, albeit critical, analysis of the professional planner's approach to urban problem solving and suggests reasons why this approach has failed to achieve even minimal success.

The first chapter, "Planning and the Critique of Urban Development", briefly describes some of the perceptions of the urban environment that have guided the professional during the past few decades. These perceptions seem to emanate from the somewhat aristocratic, anti-middle- and anti-lower-class prejudices evident in American intellectual thought since the turn of the century. They clearly illustrate an abiding faith in physical determinism and a consequent willingness on the part of the professional planner to place great stock in the notion that well-designed neighborhoods make good people.

The planner's abiding faith in determinism has been linked to an uncritical acceptance of three other isms—political separatism, logical positivism, and, as indicated in the preface, rationalism. The second chapter, "The Planner, General Planning, and the City," suggests that this philosophical stance has given rise to a set of planning tools curiously inappropriate to the complex and diverse social, economic, and environmental difficulties faced by most cities.

The professional planner has found himself unable to cope with or contribute on a sustained and meaningful basis to policy and program discussions concerning urban growth and redevelopment. As implied in the third chapter, "New Communities and Public Policy," he has endorsed, uncritically, the rhetoric of the past ten years, associated with New Towns. Unfortunately, in the process, he has abdicated any real responsibility for critically analyzing the real merits and demerits of New Towns—particularly as these merits and demerits relate to the majority of Americans who will continue to live in suburban areas and the poor who will continue to live in rural enclaves or cities.

Generally the planner has limited his contribution to federal urban policy to delivering papers at conferences or writing articles for journals. As indicated in the fourth paper, "Federal Existentialism, Planning, and Social Change," only a few ventursome planners have found themselves able to feel comfortable with or accommodate to the existential quality of the federal world. Most find their quest for order and neatness at odds with the necessity for reflecting diverse, often competing interests and priorities in federal planning. Similarly, most cannot adjust their corporate or utilitarian preceptions of public decision making to the reality of the federal decision-making process—to the tradeoffs and gaming reflected at times in federal policy making.

1

PLANNING
AND THE CRITIQUE
OF URBAN DEVELOPMENT

Americans have always been ambivalent about cities and about the life of big cities in particular. At its outset, and throughout its great period of western settlement, the country regarded itself as a garden—the garden of the world—even though its settlement was being carried forward by the railroad. And even though the onset of industrialism and the growth of the cities transformed the garden of the world into a land of machine-produced plenty, mechanical agents of change have always been seen somehow as alien presences.[1] This has been especially true for intellectuals, or at least most consistently and articulately so. From Jefferson to Emerson to Dewey—whose philosophy in a sense celebrates the pluralism of American urban life—the basic attitude toward cities can be summarized by John Dewey's statement: "Unless local communal life can be restored, the public cannot resolve its most urgent problem to find and identify itself."

Such general intellectual discontent has taken increasingly specific form in the writings and work of urban critics and planners who have insisted that the existing patterns of urban development lack meaning and order, and destroy community. Taken together, their work forms a critique whose adherents by now range from the academy to the mass media to government. Because of its broad and articulate base of support, this critique has strongly influenced the development of the new communities. It has helped create an

---

This chapter originally appeared in Edward Eichler and Marshall Kaplan, The Community Builders (Berkeley: University of California Press, 1970), pp. 1-10.

atmosphere in which the objectives of the new communities are seen
as matters of public concern. More directly, the critique has provided
many of the builders with the terms they use to express what they are
doing and why. Most significantly, it has provided several of them with
one of the ruling motives behind their activity.

The critique of urban development is thus part of the ground out
of which the new communities have grown. This chapter takes a look
at its foremost features, chiefly as seen through the words of its
creators.

EBENEZER HOWARD AND THE GARDEN CITY

Modern American thought about the defects of contemporary
urban life and the social organizations in which these defects could
be righted, begins with an Englishman. Ebenezer Howard, writing in
the last decade of the nineteenth century, based his view of contemporary urban life on an analysis of the waste and disorganization which
the industrial revolution had brought to Europe's major cities. Howard
saw urban centers growing larger and larger and felt that this growth
would intensify all the problems of the city and make life there less
and less humane. In his book, Tomorrow: A Peaceful Path to Real
Reform,[2] first published in 1898, Howard proposed that the English
government establish a series of small, self-sufficient towns under
public control. The population of each was to approximate 30,000.
By owning the land, the town could profit from the appreciation in
land value and thus finance local services. The towns would be connected by transportation systems to the country's major urban center,
London, and would be designed to catch London's "over-spill." Each
town would be protected from encroachment (and prevented from expanding) by a permanent greenbelt circumscribing its borders.

Howard did not conceive of the new towns he proposed as elements
that in themselves would right the defects of city life. Rather he saw
a symbiotic relationship between city and suburb:

> There are in reality not only, as is so constantly assumed,
> two alternatives—town life and country life—but a third
> alternative in which all the advantages of the most ener-
> getic and active town life, with all the beauty and delight
> of the country, may be secured in perfect combination;
> and the certainty of being able to live this life will be the
> magnet which will produce the effect for which we are all
> striving—the spontaneous movement of the people from
> our crowded cities to the bosom of our kindly mother
> earth, at once the source of life, of happiness, of wealth,
> and of power.[3]

Howard's concept of the Garden City found many adherents in the United States, one of the earliest being Patrick Geddes. In Cities in Evolution, written a decade after Howard's work, Geddes took the Garden City concept and proposed such towns as part of regional plans. The first realization of Howard's concept in England came in 1904 with the developments of Letchwork (designed by Barry Parker and Raymond Unwin) and Welwyn (Unwin). The concept as modified by Geddes did not become a reality in the United States for almost another thirty years. During this period, it was kept alive by the work of the Regional Planning Association, a New York organization formed to encourage area-wide planning. Its brilliant list of members included Lewis Mumford (who had been a student of Geddes), Stuart Chase, Catherine Bauer, Clarence Stein, and Henry Wright.

With the advent of the depression, the Federal government (as well as many private, local groups) made a concerted effort to shift people from cities to adjoining rural areas; the government established over one hundred developments, most of them intended as experiments in non-urban (in a manner of speaking, even anti-urban) living. Their prime purpose was either to attract people "back to the land" or to encourage subsistence farming.

During Roosevelt's second term, the government's Resettlement Administration began to develop three new communities on the basis of Geddes' modification of Howard. These communities were the "greenbelt" towns: Greenbelt, Maryland; Greenhills, Cincinnati; and Greendale, Milwaukee. With the exception of Stein's Radburn, they constitute the only major attempt to establish English-style garden cities in America. The towns were each to have had a population of up to 10,000 and a full range of community facilities—schools, hospitals, cultural centers, and so forth. The Resettlement Administration, and particularly its Administrator, Rexford Tugwell, saw the towns as a way to meet the challenges of suburban growth and, at the same time, provide lower-income families with new and better housing.

With the end of the depression, and the start of the war, this bold experiment in public planning came to an end. The greenbelt towns were never completed and were engulfed by subsequent urbanization. Yet even as they stand today, shadows of an unrealized hope, they remain a testimonial to Tugwell's far-reaching vision.

THE REGIONAL MESS

The urban-development critique, considered as a whole, is a recoil of horror and outrage at what is seen as urbanization run wild. The language often runs to science-fiction images of devastation and monstrous growths. A typical example comes from the California

architect, Richard Neutra, in an analysis with the dark title, Survival
Through Design. Neutra asks: "Must we remain victims, strangled
and suffocated by our own design which has surrounded us with man-
devouring metropolises, drab small towns manifesting a lack of order
devastating to the soul, blighted countrysides along railroad tracks
and highways, studded with petty mere utility structures shaded by
telephone poles and scented by gasoline fumes?"[4] Similarly, Lewis
Mumford speaks of the failure to divide its [the metropolis'] social
chromosomes and split up into new cells, each bearing some portion
of the original inheritance, the city continues to grow inorganically,
indeed cancerously, by a continuous breaking down of old tissues, and
an overgrowth of formless tissue.[5] Probably the most specific formulation of the development critique's basic response to the contemporary
situation comes from Peter Blake's book, God's Own Junkyard, written
in 1964. Blake, editor of Architectural Forum, says: ". . . we are
about to turn this beautiful inheritance [the American landscape] into
the biggest slum on the face of the earth. 'The mess that is man-made
America,' as a British magazine has called it, is a disgrace of such
vast proportions that only a concerted national effort can hope to return
physical America to the community of civilized nations."[6]

According to the critique, nothing escapes the brutal marks of
the urbanization process, which begins in the old central cities. In
the words of Senator Harrison Williams of New Jersey: "The impact
of this decentralization of downtown areas is plain to see. Business
wilts in the traffic congestion, property values sink, tax revenue
declines, slums multiply and the need for a larger urban renewal
program intensifies."[7] The great functions of the city are also
seriously weakened. From another national magazine, House and
Home: "Suburban sprawl negates and frustrates the purpose of cities
which is to let more people live and work close together and so utilize
and enjoy the maximum efficiency of community facilities and community enterprises, with easy access and cheap distribution."[8]

Not only the city suffers, but the area around it as well. Between
the city and the suburb, aesthetic damage is coupled with a new kind
of emotional pressure. Senator Williams again: "Frenzied traffic
makes driving an obstacle race, and the greed of the subdividers
disfigures the city's natural beauty."[9] There is also economic waste.
From a brochure describing the situation in California in 1962,
"California, Going, Going . . ." issued by California Tomorrow, a
non-profit educational institution: ". . . this state's supremely attrac-
tive resources of land, air and water are being defiled by disorderly,
unsightly intrusions of subdivisions, cars, roads, parking spaces,
sewage, exhaust, strip development, suburbs—sloppy, sleasy, slovenly,
slipshod semi-cities."[10] The waste and economic inefficiency extend
even to the developments. William Whyte, one of the earliest students

of contemporary suburbia, details the point in his study, The Exploding Metropolis: "Where the new developments are scattered at random in the outlaying areas, the costs of providing services becomes excruciating. There is not only the cost of running sewers and water mains and storm drains out to Happy Acres but much more road, per family served, has to be paved and maintained. . . . Sprawl also means low volume utility operation for the amount of installation involved."[11]

But what of the developments themselves? What are they like? And how do their residents fare? The critique sees no relief here either. A best-seller on conditions in the new suburbia, John Keats' The Crack in the Picture Window, describes the life it offers in these terms: ". . . a housing development cannot be called a community, for what word implies a balanced society of men, women and children wherein work and pleasure are found and the needs of all the society's members are several. Housing developments offer no employment and as a general rule lack recreational areas, churches, schools or other cohesive influences."[12]

E. A. Gutkind, discussing suburbia in his book, The Expanding Environment, summons up all the apocalyptic horror of the urban-development critique in the following statement:

> The last vestiges of a community have disappeared. They are hardly anything else than an agglomeration of innumerable and isolated details, of human atoms, and rows of boxes, called houses, interspersed between the industries. It is a total victory of a laissez faire insensibility and recklessness over organic growth and even over organized development.[13]

HOW DID IT HAPPEN?

The urban-development critique lists many factors that have contributed to this deplorable situation—among them, rising levels of income, population growth, and the increased mobility provided by the automobile. But to this group of critics, none of these factors seems fundamental; what brought the country to its present pass was speculation and misguided, piecemeal Federal policies. The writings of the urban critique strike this note again and again. Typical references can be gleaned from Senator Williams' testimony, Arthur Gallion's The Urban Pattern, William Whyte's The Exploding Metropolis, and so on. Probably the most concise formulation of the argument appears in Peter Blake's God's Own Junkyard.

Suburbia got that way for two simple reasons: first, because the developers who built it are, fundamentally, no
different from manufacturers of any other mass produced
product: they standardize the product, package it, arrange
for rapid distribution and easy financing and sell it off the
shelf as fast as they can. And, second, because the Federal
government, through FHA and other agencies set up to cope
with the serious housing shortages that arose after World
War II, has imposed a bureaucratic straight jacket on the
design of most new houses, on the placement of houses on
individual lots, on landscaping, on street planning, and on
just about everything else that gives suburbia its "waste-
land" appearance.[14]

In short, the disastrous sprawl of the past twenty years is seen
as the product of the merchant builder and the government bureaucrat
together, each in his own way responding only to the immediate needs
of the moment.

WHAT IS THE CURE?

There are any number of proposals in the different writings of
the urban-development critique as to how future urbanization should
proceed and the nature of goals at which it should aim. Here is a
small sampling from as many authors as there are quotations. It will
be clear that they are all part of one extended discussion.

We are going to have to relate the adequate house of our
future to the community in which it will stand.[15]

. . . the metropolis should be "imageable." That is,
it should be visually vivid and well structured; its component parts should be easily recognized and easily interrelated. This objective would encourage the use of intensive centers, variety, sharp gain, and a differentiated but
well patterned flow system.[16]

We could begin to establish and enforce statewide
standards for the location and development of our cities to
make sure that they are reasonably compact, widely separated by open space, served by suitable transportation,
and balanced enough to minimize the need for long distance
cross commuting, whether to jobs or to leisure time facilities.[17]

In short, it makes eminently good economic sense
for suburbia to encourage a mixture of building types, if
only to reduce the cost of public schools. Quite obviously,
it makes just as good economic sense to encourage the
concentration of buildings on the one hand, and the open
park land on the other, so as to reduce the length of roads
and utilities, and the cost of policing or maintaining them.[18]

Common to all these proposals is one central idea: that future
developments should be conceived in terms of wholes—that they be
determined on the basis of essential physical, social, economic, and
human needs. Future development, in other words, must be thoroughly
planned.

To the urban-development critique the past twenty years has
been a period of pernicious individualism and destructive chaos.
Against these forces, the critique opposes the rational mind and its
ability to plan. To the critique, it is planning—executed from a sufficiently high level of comprehensiveness—that will build Utopia.

This relentless and seemingly thorough-going critique was
bound to influence men whose general interest in civic affairs was
already high. For owners of large parcels of land, such as Janss
and Irvine (developers of Janss/Conejo and Irvine Ranch, respectively)
for inheritors of wealth accumulated through real-estate ventures,
such as Robert Simon (the developer of Reston); and for some who had
earned their own fortunes in a field related to real estate, as had
James Rouse (the developer of Columbia)—the chance to shape a new
life style in suburbia was irresistible. At the same time, such men
are products of a culture which esteems those who make a profit.
Thus, they would not just "create better communities," but would
earn money doing it. The great aim of the community builders is to
prove that the profit motive can be harnessed to meet head on the
deficiencies exposed by the critique of urban development.

As the planning for new communities proceeded, however, con-
flicts arose between the goals of the planners and the profit motive.
Most often, the conflict arose over how to deal with the planners'
enemy, the automobile. In his book, The Heart of our Cities, architect
Victor Gruen, whose firm drew the plans of at least six new communities, describes his concept of the properly designed metropolis:

The low densities in the neighborhoods (50 persons
per gross acre) are considerably higher than those we
find in our sprawling suburban areas . . .
Within each of the neighborhoods, within the community centers, the town centers, the city centers and the
various nuclei of Metrocenter, there will be a pattern of

pedestrian walks and plazas, and this pattern will extend
into the green areas surrounding them, in order to connect
various nuclei with each other. . . .
    Local vehicular roads and highways . . . related to
each one of the nuclei, will be established as loop roads
surrounding each nucleus and connecting up to car storage
facilities located on the fringe of each nucleus in the form
of underground or multiple-deck garages. In a neighborhood, for example, garages will not be attached to every
residence. [19]

Gruen, like many other urban critics and planners, apparently
believes either that most suburbanites do not really want to rely on
automobiles or that they should be forced to adopt another style of
life. But confronted with early plans for relatively high-density
neighborhoods in which parking was separated from the individual
dwelling, community builders consistently decided that most of their
prospective customers would continue to demand low-density, detached
houses with attached garages.

What underlies this conflict seems to be the planners' antipathy
for the American middle class and a yearning for aristocratic taste
and values: "All this [suburbia]," writes Lewis Mumford, "is a far
cry from the aristocratic enjoyment of visual space that provided the
late Baroque city with open squares and circles and long vistas for
carriage drives down tree lined avenues."[20] The businessmen under-
taking new communities may share this view, but time and again they
have been forced to remind themselves and their planners that this
very middle class is the market to which their projects must appeal.

Proponents of planning have come more and more to see planning
as a dynamic process, which enables decision-makers to be better
prepared to cope with exigencies as they arise. Too often the planning
process for new communities has been the opposite. It has been an
attempt to bind the community builder and the occupants of new communities to a preconceived set of notions about what suburban life ought
to be. Much of this book will illustrate the difficulties which arise
under such conditions.

NOTES

1. See Leo Marx, The Machine in the Garden (New York:
Oxford University Press, 1964) for a penetrating discussion of the
pastoral ideal in America, both in the general consciousness and in
American literature—and how this ideal responded to the coming of the
machine.

2. The book was later slightly revised and published in a second edition with the title changed to Garden Cities of Tomorrow (London: S. Sonnenschein, 1902).

3. Ebenezer Howard, Garden Cities of Tomorrow (London: Faber and Faber, 1914), pp. 45-46.

4. Richard Neutra, Survival Through Design (New York: Oxford University Press, 1954).

5. Lewis Mumford, The City in History (New York: Harcourt, Brace, and World, 1961), p. 543.

6. Peter Blake, God's Own Junkyard (New York: Holt, Rinehart, and Winston, 1964), p. 8.

7. Senator Harrison Williams, U.S. Senate Committee on Banking and Currency, 87th Congress, 1st Session, Hearings, Housing Legislation of 1961.

8. "Land," House and Home, XVIII, 2 (August 1960), 114.

9. Ibid.

10. Samuel E. Wood and Alfred E. Heller, "California, Going, Going . . ." (Sacramento, Calif.: California Tomorrow, 1962).

11. William Whyte, The Exploding Metropolis, (Garden City, N.Y.: Anchor Books, 1958), p. 122.

12. John Keats, The Crack in the Picture Window (Boston: Houghton Mifflin, 1957), Introduction, p. xvi.

13. As quoted in Keats, op. cit., p. 176.

14. Blake, op. cit., p. 17.

15. Keats, op. cit., p. 184.

16. Kevin Lynch, "The Pattern of the Metropolis," Daedalus, XC, 1 Journal of the American Academy of Arts and Sciences, (Winter 1961), 94.

17. Samuel E. Wood and Alfred E. Heller, Phantom Cities of California, (Sacramento, Calif.: California Tomorrow, 1963), pp. 65-66.

18. Blake, op. cit., p. 19.

19. Victor Gruen, The Heart of Our Cities (New York: Simon & Schuster, 1964), pp. 274, 277-278.

20. Mumford, op cit., p. 503.

CHAPTER

2

THE PLANNER,
GENERAL PLANNING,
AND THE CITY

Speaking of city planners, the eminent sociologist David Reisman writes, "they comprise perhaps the most important professional group to become reasonably weary of cultural definitions that are systematically trotted out to rationalize the inadequacies of city life today, for the well-to-do as well as for the poor. With their imagination and bounteous approach they have become to some extent, the guardians of our liberal and progressive political tradition."[1] Certainly there is accumulating evidence, that individual planners, planning departments, and the professions are awaking to realities of urban life. Yet, the above statement needs to be tempered by any realistic appraisal of the field. Until recently, our history is one of non-involvement by choice in the "politics of a city," our philosophy is steeped in an errant logical positivism, our marching orders have been city beautiful, city practical, city economic, and only recently city social.

More than 12 years ago, at an AIP Conference, Catherine Bauer Wurster admonished planners to understand the social effects of their physical plans and to leave behind their bundling board attitude which separates physical and social planning.[2] Yet, even to this day with very few exceptions physical plans avoid the subject of race, do not take cognizance of the needs of the aged, the poor, and do not reflect the emerging effect of automation on the inhabitants of cities. This is odd in a profession whose beginnings are steeped in physical determinism.

This chapter originally appeared in Land Economics Journal, August 1964, pp. 295-302.

It is feared that if city planners do not begin to discard some of their old obsolete ideas of the city—ideas which are reflected in their plans—then planners will play only a tangential role in the creation of the new urban environment.

Planners have too often seen the city through the eyes of the nominalist as a collection of neat functions prescribed by rigid physical dimensions. They have concentrated too long on urban form as an abstraction, rather than the relation of urban form to the lives, not of a generic homogenaic population, but of the Negro, the single person, the aged, the divorcee and widowed. They have found it easier to accept the image of a static city with definite edges and a core than to look at the complexities relative to realities of American cities. In accepting this static image we have often recommended programs which in fitting our image took the heat from the melting pot. What are these realities? What is unique to the American experience? What is the future of the American city? Where does the planner fit in?

URBAN REALITIES

Opprobriums such as slurb, sprawl, scatteration, gray areas, blight have been utilized to describe the effects of the urbanization process. In effect, those vivid terms are but symbolic of the changing and dynamic patterns witnessed in the urban scene. During the ten-year period from 1950 to 1960 the number of residents living in urban areas increased by almost 29,000,000, bringing the total to 125,000,000 or 70% of the Nation's populace. Within this same span of years, nearly 5,000,000 additional acres were brought under the umbrella of urban areas.

Synonymous with the growth in numbers of urban residents has been the noticeable decline of rural areas. Within urban areas we have noticed the tremendous dispersion of population. Out from central cities have moved the middle- and upper-class whites. These people have been replaced by the poor, the aged, and most often the Negro. The 22 largest cities in the United States portrayed a gain of over 2,150,000 nonwhite residents between 1950 to 1960 while losing over 1,120,000 whites. In ten of these major urban complexes, nonwhite residents comprised over one fourth of the total populace while in Washington, D. C. the "minority" approximates 60 percent of inhabitants of the city. Ample statistics are also available which indicate a complementary rise in the numbers of elderly and low income households in central cities.

Unable to compete in the housing market, excluded from partic-ipation in the style or way of life changes in American society, unable to participate fully in the visible affluence on the American scene, these new urban residents are increasingly becoming alienated from the mainstream of life in the Nation. More often then not their homes are substantially over-crowded and concentrated in "decaying or segregated" areas.

The influx of the low income and the minority household to the cities has been, as mentioned above, complemented by an exodus of the more affluent whites. Cities find themselves in a bind. With a diminishing tax base they are faced with an aging and often outmoded public infrastructure. In the terms of the economist "external economies" such as good schools, parks, and open space needed to retain the well and almost well-to-do are absent. A wide range of housing types and prices is fast disappearing, leaving the city to the very poor or the very rich. Additionally, cities find themselves unable to compete with fringe areas for industry. With industrial dispersion, lower income families face either longer journey's to work or reduced employment opportunities. In either case their already limited incomes are further diminished, their opportunity span reduced.

Despite periodic warnings the great mass of Americans seem to be unconcerned about the future of our cities. The flight to the suburbs continues, for in the suburbs "the privileged white can, in fact, build a wall around his cultural standards and social class mores by utilizing the economic barriers of building costs, occupancy standards, tax rates, and commuting costs."[3] Dr. Raymond Vernon sums up the dilemma of those of us who decry current urban developments, when he states, "for all the chorus of protests, however, most Americans seem strongly unaroused. Each year they buy a few hundred-thousand picture windows, seed a few hundred-thousand lawns. The decay of the central city barely concerns them . . . . What I shall contend with in substance is that the clear majority of Americans who live in urban areas look on their life-time experience as one of progress and improvement, not as one of retrogression."[4]

This progress and improvement—this mobility—should be facilitated by life in the city. The view of the American city as a take-off point launching the new immigrants into the dominant middle-class America remains a valid one. "Doing this—bringing people from society's backwaters into the mainstream of American life—has always been the principal business, and the principal glory of the American city."[5] Yet evidence is accumulating that cities are not fulfilling this urbanizing function for the new Negro and low income in-migrant. Furthermore, with forecasts of increased automation in industry requiring a greater expertise and educational level, as well as fewer employees, one cannot find comfort in traditional American optimism relative to the economic mobility of the lower income individual. It is probable that, unless a solution is found, both the absolute and relative number of low income people will increase. It is also probable that a heavier incidence of the low income household will continue to be found among the Negro. Both the low-income white and the low-income Negro will find, because of market factors, cultural factors, and discrimination, cities their principal abode. One might also suggest that today's dilemma regarding racial discrimination will be compounded, if not submerged by class prejudices. Manifestations of this are already appearing and are imaged by the city-suburb dichotomy.

THE ROLE OF THE PLANNER IN URBAN SOCIETY
AND THE GENERAL PLAN APPROACH

In general, most early devotees of city planning in America defined planning in relation to general physical objectives rather than as a process encompassing certain generic steps common to all forms of decision-making. Planning was usually for something or led to something. Since planning was (and is) struggling to prove its inherent worth to communities, this attempt to identify it with general community desires probably was the proper strategy for its adherents to employ. After all, it is easier to talk about relieving congestion than about goal formulation.

Recently, however, perhaps indicating that city planning is at last an acceptable profession, much more thought has been given to planning as a process. It might be expected that after a realization that the word physical, economic, or social attached to the word planning merely clothes the latter with flexible boundaries, that only the process is absolute, a closer linkage between the different academic and professional specializations, would have occurred. Yet, this has not happened.

Once academicians and practioners began to think of planning as a process, the various parts of the process were abstracted out and defined rather carefully. For example, "the relationship of design for physical development to the social and economic aspects of urban planning may be clarified by making a distinction between the four phases of the planning process: 1) goal formulation; 2) survey and analyses; 3) plan preparation; and 4) plan effectuation,"[6] or "in its essential characteristics the planning approach to problem-solving is largely neutral with respect to subject matter, and although it cannot work with specific goals predetermined, it is intrinsically normative. By its very nature, the planning task is oriented to choosing among alternative values—to evaluating alternative multi-goal sets, as these goals appear in a hierarchal and temporal continuum of ends-means."[7]

The planning approach outlined above is normally referred to as
the ends-means approach. In theory and practice it is quite comprehensive, calling for the evaluation of goals, actions, and consequences
within the framework of the total urban area. An example of the
product of this approach is the general plan—a document which usually
states long-run (20-30 years) development goals and a very tenuous
set of actions to achieve them.

Since an integrated comprehensive goal system is posited as an
ideal, the list of goals enumerated, given urban realities described
earlier, must be long range and reduced to a community-wide jointly
shared value base (amenity, beauty, etc.). Furthermore, given their
somewhat amorphous nature, goals cannot be rated cardinally or
ordinally nor can they realistically differentiate between geographical
areas or differential population characteristics. In effect, only in the
distant future can the level of comprehensiveness posited be defined;
for the type of goal formulation described above indeed premises a
closed system and only apart from the existing urban scene can such
a system be derived.

This proclivity for the Rational or Comprehensive method of
decision-making neglects the facts of urban life. Decisions in urban
society are not made in this manner. Therefore, resultant goals
achieved through this process are, in order to approximate consensus,
sterile, devoid of real meaning, and quite difficult to translate into
realizable programs.

Additionally, "although such an approach can be described, it
cannot be practiced except for relatively simple problems and even
then only in a somewhat modified form. It assumes intellectual
capacities and sources of information that men simply do not possess
and it is even more absurd as an approach to policy when the time
and money that can be allocated to a policy problem is limited, as is
always the case."[8] That urban areas are pluralistic in demographic
composition, that decision-making resembles a game with many
players, many goal systems, and many strategies is accepted, at
least verbally, by the profession. Yet, a void exists between verbal
expression and practicing reality.

Selection of values, goals and empirical analyses cannot be
separated from one another. Both must be done incrementally for
decisions are made incrementally. The "test" of good policy, then,
is that the various doers agree on that policy without necessarily
agreeing on a long-range goal structure. Once the planner realizes
this, he can participate in the process of decision-making. He can
propose a strategy for development which encompasses limited objectives, recognizes political realities and differentiates between and
among peoples and area. Rather than shy away from social problems,
social problems will become the quid pro quo of planning for the

physical environment. The nearest statement by a professional planner of this view emanated from Martin Meyerson in 1956:

> Yet the framework required by the people who make some
> of the key decisions for both private and public community
> development is not provided by project planning. Nor is
> the urgency of these decisions met by the kind of long-
> range comprehensive planning we usually do. I have con-
> cluded that a middle ground is needed. An intermediate
> set of planning functions must be performed on a sus-
> tained, on-going basis to provide a framework[9] . . .
> (for decision-making).

Meyerson lists the following as new functions for the planner: (1)
central intelligence; (2) pulse taking; (3) policy clarification; (4) detailed development plan, and (5) feedback review.

In defining a role for planners, we should realize that urbanization will continue. Rather than containment, the process needs
direction. Rather than attempts to slow it down, it should be speeded
up thus permitting the distribution of benefits to lower income people.
Existing cities, as Bebout states, will play a vital role in this process,
serving "the rest of society at present and for the immediate future
as a combination Ellis Island and training school for the receipt,
training and ultimate transshipment to the suburbs of under privileged
in-migrants."[10] Meeting this role effectively offers hope that cities
can be effectively redeveloped over time, for as low-income families
and Negroes take their place in the wider process of urbanization,
political and economic pressures will be removed which presently
prohibit effective renewal of physical plants and structures. In recognizing this prime aspect of cities, planners recognize the interrela-
tionship between development and redevelopment.

Implicit in seeing the city as a place where acculturation is to
take place, is a commitment to providing a wider number of choices
relative to housing, environment, and employment opportunities to
those presently disenfranchised. I would say that this should be one
of the prime objectives of the city planner: "having been assigned
responsibility for guiding land use patterns, we seek then to induce
those patterns that will maximize the accessibility of the cities'
residents to the broad range of opportunities for interaction that
advanced civilization opens to them."[11]

Do the concepts of the city and the planning process as expressed
above call for revision of the planners traditional operational processes? The answer to this, despite the difficulties involved, is yes and
the first place to start is with the general plan. In a dynamic, mobile
urban society, where politics is at best incremental and serves as a

safety value for the strivings of different groups, long range general plans emphasizing physical form in terms of defined edges and internal structure, serve mainly as a salutory device at budget time. In essence, the political and administrative framework within which the planner operates encourages instability while the traditional two-dimensional, twenty- to fifty-year plan is a static concept and breathes stability. Continued production of "general plans" which concentrate on long-term, esoteric (esoteric to the politician, the administrator, the developer) goals will place the profession outside the confidence of decision makers. Attempts to create comprehensive areawide two-dimensional design schemes are doomed to failure, because they are not attuned to the politics of mutual adjustment, bargaining and compromise.

To date, as implied, the planning process and the resultant product has concentrated on the whole city, on the generic, on the corporate and communal aspects of the city neglecting the hetero-geneous character of the people and neighborhoods. The meaning of community has become something different from the individuals who reside in it. Objectives expressed in the general plan of one city could be easily transferred to any other city. This acceptance by the planner of a somewhat organismic concept of community, one in which really only middle-class values were acceptable, impeded an under-standing of the city and negated his role in the decision-making process.

Abstraction is a necessary tool toward understanding a complex field of data. It is also useful in alluding to key elements in a generic process. Yet, when the abstractor in this case the planner, permits the abstraction to substitute for reality, in effect to become a normative model for action, then danger lurks.

Allow me to suggest a substitute for the general plan approach. Recognizing the pluralistic nature of our cities as well as the incre-mental nature of our political system, the planners should not attempt to abstract a complete set of urban values, nor will he need to evalu-ate all the consequences of all alternatives. Paralleling, the way decisions are made, the planners will restrict their attention to fewer alternative policies.

The implications of the above are many. Long range definitive design plans encompassing whole urban areas should become an in-ternal office exercise, an envelope for ideas, a model referred to for comparisons—replaced by development and redevelopment policies limited both in scale, area and time span. Emphasis ought to be on planning as a resource allocation process with criteria prepared by the planner to assist in the dispersion of public goods and the direction of private growth. Equal treatment in terms of time or expenditures will not be available to all areas of the urban complex. Problem areas will be identified by the planner. Given limited resources, limited choices or alternatives will be presented to the community. Assuming urban areas are to serve as a training ground for the disadvantaged, if social pathologies are identified in the planning process, and socio-economic and physical costs of slum or ghetto areas are fed into benefit-cost analysis, we could assume recommendations by the planner for greater inputs into disadvantaged areas.

Reversal of the historical pattern which saw recommendations proposed by the planner that were indifferent to the particular characteristics of one area and one group as compared to another, and which focused on the use of land not on the inhabitants of that land, will follow a priori after acceptance of planning as a policy-oriented process. Emanating from a commitment to an environment within which no one shall be denied access to items dispersed by the public or offered in the market place, will come criteria to be utilized in resource allocation and analyses of development policies.

COMMUNITY PARTICIPATION

In order to gain political acceptance of proposals as well as a feedback relative to potential consequences, the planner must continue to experiment in the area of community participation. Particularly in racially compact and disadvantaged areas, a strong community network between the planned for and the planner will be useful to both participants. If subculture is not to be used as a "self-frustrating defense against a sense of inferiority," as a barrier towards involvement in general community improvement programs, and as an excuse for the imprisonment of unused potential, then a sense of belonging to a wider community must be nourished. Direct involvement in the planning process will be an embryonic step in this direction. Involvement will also serve the planner in that he will gain a new and needed insight into the pluralism of urban society and into the richness in the variety of its cultures.

This continued commitment to increasing community participation in the planning process will (1) enable the general community to understand the need for planning; (2) develop better liaison between citizen and planner pertaining to the rehabilitation process; and (3) facilitate understanding of those residents in renewal areas relative to displacement needs.

Concomitant with any realistic citizen participation program is the need to develop community leadership. Both programs are necessary to lessen the adverse social impacts and improve human adjustments to urban living. Translated into physical dimensions, community improvement programs should include neighborhood service centers

where social and physical services can be joined at the neighborhood
level. Cities should experiment with new modes of housing and community living geared to specific urban populations bypassed in the
urbanizing process—skid row, broken families, single people.

PLANNING ORGANIZATION

Departure from the general plan concept and acceptance of the
approach to planning defined in this paper suggest a much closer
relationship between physical and social planning. While there is not
a one-to-one ratio relative to the effect the physical environment has
on social behavior, complex cause and effect relationships do exist.

Social planning can make a significant contribution to the welfare of urban residents by the careful analyses of the impact of physical
changes on human beings. If planning for the physical environment
is thought of as instrumental to the achievement of social ends, then
the artificial barriers created by nomenclature such as social and
physical will be broken.

Several approaches can be utilized to integrate social and physical planning: (One) Research is needed on the cause and effect
relationships relative to the physical environment and human development. Joint teams of behavioral psychiatrists, sociologists, planners,
and the design professions should engage in continuous basic and
applied research pertaining to the extent to which micro and macro
spatial relationships and urban forms influence the individual and
groups.

(Two) Experimentation with changes in the organizational framework within which the planner is located seem appropriate. Two or
three structural adaptations might be suggested: (a) Within a planning
department itself an assistant director might be appointed to assume
responsibility for liaison with social welfare and planning agencies.
(b) Psychiatrists and sociologists should be added as a normal
complement to a planning department either as staff or advisors.
These individuals should participate in the continuing planning process of the agency in question. (c) Within the chief executive's office
(be he a city manager or mayor depending on the communities' organizational structure) there might be located an individual to serve as
a social welfare coordinator. It would be his role to review and coordinate the recommendations and activities of line and staff agencies
relative to social problems.

In this paper, I have suggested several departures from current
planning practices. These proposals emanate from one deeply concerned with the problems of central cities and their inhabitants.
Planners have made important contributions to improving urban life.

To be satisfied, however, with past accomplishments is not enough. We must be aware of our own limitations if we are to contribute significantly to the solution of growing future needs. As Mel Webber stated, "the city planners who have earned our highest respect are those whose revisions of betterment become epidemic in these communities, raising civic aspirations and forcing solutions of specific problems."[12]

NOTES

1. David Riesman, The Lonely Crowd (New York: Doubleday, 1953), p. 348.

2. Catherine Bauer Wurster, "The Increasing Social Responsibility of the City Planner," a speech before the Annual Meeting of the American Institute of Planners, March 3, 1950.

3. John W. Dyckman, "Control of Land Development and Urbanization in California," Housing in California (San Francisco: Governor's Advisory Commission on Housing Problems, 1963), p. 310.

4. Raymond Vernon, The Myths and Reality of Our Urban Problem (Cambridge, Mass.: Joint Center for Urban Studies, 1962), p. 1.

5. Charles Silberman, "The City and the Negro," Fortune Magazine, March 1962, p. 89.

6. Frederick J. Adams, Urban Planning Education in the United States (New York: Bettman Foundation, 1954), p. 1.

7. Melvin M. Webber, "The Prospects of Policies Planning," in Leonard Duhl, ed. The Urban Condition (New York: Basic Books, 1963), p. 320.

8. Charles E. Lindblom, "The Science of Muddling Through," Public Administration Review, XIX,2 (1959), p. 80.

9. Martin Meyerson, "Building the Middle Range Bridge for Comprehensive Planning," Journal of the American Institute of Planners, Spring 1956, p. 58.

10. John Bebout and Harry C. Bredemeier, "American Cities as Social Systems," Journal of the American Institute of Planners, May 1963, p. 68.

11. Melvin Webber, "Comprehensive Planning and Social Responsibility," draft paper, Planning Policy Conference, Washington, D.C., February 22, 1964, p. 3.

12. Webber, loc. cit., p. 8.

CHAPTER

3

NEW COMMUNITIES
AND PUBLIC POLICY

In 1963 the California Housing report proposed a two-fold program to help initiate new communities—state loans to community builders or direct purchase of land by the state. In 1964 and 1965 the Johnson Administration asked Congress for authorization to make loans either to private sponsors or to the states for the same purpose.[1] None of these measures was enacted, but all were based on the thesis that underlay the Community Development Project—that there are serious problems in American society which can be attacked by a new method of developing land at the fringe of metropolitan areas. The thesis held further that large areas of such fringe land should be planned and developed by a single entity.

This is the belief shared by the authors when they undertook this project to try and devise one or more demonstrations which would act as a catalyst in spurring changes in public and private policies. Now, research and reflection has produced quite the contrary view—that community building, even with public aid or under public sponsorship, can do little to solve the serious problems confronting American society. This sharp about-face is due in part to a changed conception of what constitutes a serious problem and in part to a changed view of the type of action appropriate for government to take. This chapter, beginning with a review of the powers available to the various levels of government, takes a detailed look at the arguments for and against government support of new communities.

This chapter originally appeared in Edward Eichler and Marshall Kaplan, The Community Builders (Berkeley: University of California Press, 1970), pp. 160-82.

THE POWERS OF GOVERNMENT

Local Government

The primary point of interaction between a community builder and government occurs at the local level, principally the county. If a local master plan of the area exists, this plan determines the uses to which the developer may put his land—residential, commercial, industrial, and so forth. If a master plan does not exist, then the local government makes its determination on the basis of a plan submitted by the developer. Beyond this, zoning ordinances specify what is permitted within each category in regard to such items as lot sizes, building heights, the portion of a site which can be covered by a building, and the ratios of on-and off-street parking. Subdivision regulations further specify street and sidewalk widths, requirements for street and sidewalk construction, maximum slopes, and so on.

As a rule community builders submit their own plans. To secure flexibility not possible under regular zoning ordinances and subdivision regulations, they try to create planned-community ordinances or use those already in existence.

The other important power of local government is to grant the right to establish a special district with authority to issue tax-exempt bonds. Normally, election to the newly created district board is determined by assessed valuation of property. Since community builders own a great deal of land and expect to develop and retain income property, they should be able to maintain control almost indefinitely.

It seems clear that local government might take certain kinds of demands in return for its cooperation with community builders. But as the previous discussion has shown, by and large no such demands have been made, except of course that community builders fulfill their plans.

The State

All of the powers of a local government are granted by the state which created it. This relationship is not analogous to the relationship between the states and the Federal government, for the latter was also a creation of the states. The United States Constitution sets forth the rules of the state-national government compact. It provides, for example, that police power (except in special and proscribed circumstances) rests with the states. Zoning and subdivision regulations are based, in turn, on the police power granted to units of local government.

As noted earlier, the Local Agencies Formation Commissions (LAFCO's) were created by the California legislature in 1964 as the result of the proliferation of local governments. Small cities, especially special districts, had been severely criticized for their inefficiency, the low turnout in district elections, and their interference with regional decision-making. In some states, such as Minnesota, such criticism has caused the state government to create a commission to pass on proposals for the creation of new local governments.

Thus a state can facilitate or inhibit community building by altering the power of local governments and the requirements leading to their formation. It could aid community builders by making the creation of small cities more difficult or even impossible, thereby removing the threat of early incorporation (which would give residents control of zoning). But it could inhibit the process by banning the creation of special districts or limiting their formation to taxing areas created and administered by city- or county-elected officials. This policy would restrict or eliminate the use of tax-exempt bonds to finance utilities and other improvements in new communities. It appears that this is precisely the policy which Maryland and Howard County followed in refusing to authorize any kind of taxing district for Columbia.

A state has also the power to react more directly to community building. It could adopt legislation removing local control over new communities and placing it instead in a special commission which would review the plans of applicants and decide which community builders are entitled to special dispensations. Of course a state also can program public works, such as freeways, water distribution, and institutions of higher learning so as to facilitate development.

A state can go even further and use its own credit and its power of eminent domain to acquire large parcels of land and finance both acquisition and site development. As in redevelopment, the state government could sell the improved sites to private corporations, with contractual restrictions upon their use. (While there is some doubt about the constitutionality of a state using the power of eminent domain to acquire raw land from one private owner and transfer it eventually to another, the courts are likely in most cases to accept the judgment of the legislature that this is a legitimate public purpose.) The ultimate state powers of condemnation and credit could be granted to a development corporation initiated by profit seeking sponsors but containing representatives of the state, the county, surrounding municipalities, and so on.

Almost any action by a state to change the nature of new communities, or to create more or less of them, would require legislation.

Such legislation is quite conceivable since it would be based on the historic state powers of establishing local governments, using eminent domain and state credit for public purposes, and building certain kinds of public facilities.

The Federal Government

The Federal government has few programs which have as their direct purpose the creation of a specific pattern of urban development. Nonetheless, a great many Federal actions influence this development.

Programs enacted to affect physical development are administered chiefly by the Housing and Home Finance Agency (HHFA) and the Bureau of Public Roads. HHFA does not deal directly with the consumer, nor does it construct or determine the location of a public facility. What it does is to provide loans, loan guarantees or insurance, and grants to junior governments and private institutions. Its programs include: low interest-rate loans to local public agencies for facilities (sewage disposal, water supply, mass transit); matching grants to states, cities, and counties for planning; loans and grants to local public agencies to construct low-rent public housing; loans and grants to local public agencies for clearance and rehabilitation of slums (urban renewal); insurance to private lenders who provide loans at (or near) market interest to home buyers or to builders of rental housing (FHA); and insurance for loans made by the Treasury through the Federal National Mortgage Association to non-profit or limited dividend corporations for the construction or rehabilitation of housing for middle-income families (earning from about $4,000 to $8,000). In addition, the Bureau of Public Roads makes matching grants (as high as 90 percent) to the states for interstate highways.

By and large these programs have had their effect only since World War II. In the great debate about their influence upon the character and pattern of urban growth, they have, at the very least, encouraged the trend towards lower densities in all land uses and the decentralization of industry and commerce. Also, they have helped to harness the housing demand pent up until after World War II and fed since then by rising incomes. Despite this, it still would be difficult for the government to administer such programs to effect dramatic changes in the density or placement of new development because the programs function indirectly—they aid only the action of other parties.

Thus Federal programs do not have a strong, direct effect on community building. Some merchant builders sell homes with FHA or VA loans, but were the government to attach any requirements which the builders saw as onerous, they could shift to conventional loan sources without drastically altering their sales rates. Public-facility loans

and planning grants have not been used because the developments are
private projects, nor has the middle-income housing program been
used even when the development could be considered eligible.
All of this is simply to say that as a practical matter, the Federal
government does not currently have much of a carrot with which to
influence community building one way or the other. Yet, it was the
Federal government (with no outside influence seeking its intervention)
which first decided to take some action. So far HHFA[2] has been
unsuccessful in its support of the proposals it derived from the California Housing Report (to provide loans to both public and private
sponsors for land acquisition and site improvements in new communities), but it is expected that the Administration will continue to press
for them. The key provisions in the bill it sponsored were as follows:
   1. FHA would insure loans for land purchase and development.
   2. The Federal National Mortgage Association would be
authorized to purchase such loans. (Private lenders might not be
willing to hold such loans even with FHA insurance).
   3. Insured loans could provide as much as 50 percent of the
cost of the land and 90 percent of the cost of site improvements, but
could not exceed 75 percent of the value as determined by the FHA
Commissioner.
   4. The maximum loan would be $25 million.
   5. The Commissioner should assure himself that the planning
would be made "effective."
   6. The Commissioner should encourage housing for low- and
moderate-income families.
   As indicated in the last chapter, the provision for such long-
term, low interest-rate (6 percent) loans to a community builder
could have a significant impact on the return he receives on his capital.
In addition, such loans would enable many firms to undertake a new
community for which sufficient funds might not otherwise be available,
from any source at any cost.

VIRTUES AND THREATS

   The general consensus on new communities has been that they
can contribute greatly to the public good but that they require (1)
financial aid, with certain strings attached, from the Federal government and (2) some added regulation by state and local government.
   It has already been noted that junior governments have the
necessary power to provide such regulation if they care to do so. But
the question is to what purpose such power should be put at any level
of government.

Since the Johnson Administration is a strong supporter of a loan program to aid new communities, it is not surprising that one can find articulate justification for the program in the statements of the government's representatives in HHFA, even though these ideas did not originate primarily from within HHFA but represent the thinking of many experts. Its most comprehensive defense is to be found in a speech given at the University of Illinois by Dr. Robert Weaver, the director of HHFA. Because of its comprehensiveness, Dr. Weaver's speech (now published in book form)3 serves as a useful basis for discussion. We wish to emphasize here that we respect Dr. Weaver as a dedicated public servant and to state that he is presenting a position developed only after consultation with a great many city planners and developers. It is this position, and not Dr. Weaver as an individual, with which the following discussion is meant to take issue.

Scatteration, Efficiency, and the Journey to Work

Many contend that new communities will decrease the journey to work as well as to other activities. It is argued that this would save public costs for transportation, utility lines, school busing etc. In addition, the residents of new communities would have the advantage of being close to a variety of facilities and services. As Weaver put it in his speech: "More rational development of the surburban areas would minimize transportation needs and utility line extensions. And, too, the development of satellite communities affording employment opportunities, as well as educational, recreational and commercial facilities, would serve the same purpose."

How are these advantages to come about? First, the supporters of new communities argue, such developments would contain higher densities than those of conventional suburbia. But the projected density for most new communities is 3 to 3.5 dwelling units per acre, which hardly indicates great compaction. Indeed, it would require density of at least triple this figure to make any major difference in utility or transportation needs than now exists. Since the 3 to 3.5 figure appears to reflect the mutual desires of house consumers, retailers, and industry, it is unlikely that a governmental agency could establish significantly higher densities, except by adopting extremely restrictive measures.

The supporters of new communities also argue that the communities offer greater opportunities for local employment, recreation, culture, and commercial activities than do other types of development. However, while such opportunities are brought about in new communities with a marginally higher degree of speed than normally, it is nonetheless the case that the development of surburban housing on fragmented parcels has consistently been followed by the appearance of industry, recreation, and commerce. In fact, one aspect of the urban development critique, and a cause also of federally financed urban renewal, is the accurate contention that central cities are losing their industry and commerce. The point is, stores and plants are relocating in the suburbs. Moreover, there is little a community builder could do to attract such facilities to his particular project, even with the aid of any of the powers now available to government.

In Great Britain, the publicly initiated new towns do serve as industrial sites, but only because there are a host of formal and informal controls regulating industrial location. Theoretically a national policy to regulate industrial settlement could be enacted in the United States (in combination with a new community, new towns, or even a new metropolis policy), but this is far more drastic action than the advocates of new communities propose or, apparently, desire. Without such an effort, however, new communities will follow the regular pattern of development. Residents will arrive first, and the growth of local commerce and industry will follow. Moreover, as in Janss/Conejo, most new residents will be traveling further to work, and to many other places, than they did before they moved. It is true that some recreation facilities are built very much earlier in new communities than they would be in other developments, but, as noted, the lakes, golf courses, and parks are more for providing symbolic investment protection for the residents than great opportunities for their enjoyment.

Finally, it has been argued that new communities would reduce utility extensions and transportation needs because the communities would develop more rapidly than do areas under fragmented ownership. At the moment there is little evidence that this is so, but here government action could make some difference. State and local governments could give zoning and other advantages to selected new communities (by constructing a freeway to them, for example, or a university campus within them). If Federal aids of this kind were passed along to the consumer in the form of lower prices, better houses, or more amenities sales would obviously be spurred.

Still, if densities are not likely to be raised, the total amount of land consumed by a new development, whether it is in a new community or not, will remain the same. Thus, those who are staggered by the fact that "the process of urbanization consumes a million acres a year,"[4] can find no consolation in the advent of new communities, with or without government aid/or control.

But what about the prevention of "scatteration" which leaves holes of undeveloped parcels of land all over the place? Isn't this a beneficial consequence of new communities? Wouldn't it reduce the cost of public facilities and services and increase services? In the short run it might, but no reliable evidence has yet turned up which projects savings of sufficient magnitude to warrant the necessary rationing of land use and selection of some land owners for such gigantic favors.

Since the prevention of scatteration or, as it sometimes is called, sprawl, is emphasized so strongly by the supporters of new communities, it might be well to consider in more detail what the terms mean, what evils come with them, and what new communities might do about them. Harvey and Clark give the following definition:

> Sprawl, measured as a moment of time, is composed of areas of essentially urban character at the urban fringe but which are scattered or strung out, or surrounded by, or adjacent to underdeveloped sites or agricultural uses. A sprawled area has a heterogeneous pattern, with an overall density less than that found in mature compact segments of the city. Sprawl areas are less dense than would be found if the areas developed for housing would be developed with discipline exercised in the assembling of jig-saw puzzles by adding pieces from the bottom up.5

The authors go on to cite the causes of sprawl, among them tax laws, zoning regulations, mortgage policies, fragmented ownership of land, and the character of land developers. Clearly community building, as it has been discussed here, eliminates some of these factors. But to what extent are such defects critical? Harvey and Clark go on to identify two fundamental aspects of sprawl which most commentators have failed to recognize.

The first is time. Sprawl usually occurs at the fringe of a rapidly growing area. It is costly to the degree to which capital must be used to install sewer and water lines, roads, and so forth earlier than if development had proceeded in a more compact manner. However, since the area is growing rapidly, the gaps will be filled in quickly and the extra costs will be minimal. As Harvey and Clark argue: "A static or very short-run view on urban development permits an exaggeration of development cost per unit, which cost may in fact be modest on a unit basis once the development is viewed as a complete entity." 6

Even more important is the second issue they raise—of who bears the extra cost, if any, of sprawl. Freeways are usually installed without regard to the specific character of urban development. Thus, the capital cost of freeways is probably unaffected by sprawl. Sprawl may increase driving time and cost, but these burdens are borne by the resident, not society. Again, most scattered projects (at least in California) must pay for the cost of longer runs for sewer and water mains. But here too, it is the resident—not society—who pays the price.

However, in some cases this situation does not obtain. Electricity and gas, for instance, are supplied to almost any site, and the costs of their distribution are reflected in general rates. Thus, all users share the burden of capital outlay. In such circumstances, a change in laws and regulations is required so that the specific users pay the cost of their locational choice without subsidy from society as a whole.

It cannot be said that new communities necessarily reduce the extra costs which supposedly come from sprawl or scatteration, for usually communities leapfrog open land and so require extensions of utility lines. From society's viewpoint, however, their value is that these burdens accrue to the land itself, in the form of lower receipts to the land owner or higher costs to the new user. In any event, if one keeps in mind the concept of time, sprawl does not seem to result in additional economic cost of great magnitude. The same can be said about esthetics, for the unsightliness of scattered development is only temporary.[7] If one is concerned not just with scatteration but also with the visual quality of developed suburbia, one really is objecting to the taste of America's middle class. We find it difficult to believe that market-oriented new communities, aided by Federal loans, will drastically alter such esthetic values.

Supporters of new communities are on fairly strong grounds when they cite greater open space as a likely consequence of new communities. To be more precise one might say that when community builders dedicate open land to a public agency or a home-owners association, the land is likely to remain largely undeveloped for a long time. When ownership is fragmented and open space is desired, the local government must purchase the land to prevent it from being used. If the government waits until surrounding land is developed, then the price it must pay becomes very high.

With community builders, however, the cost of the open land is added onto the price of the developed land. Thus, in effect, new communities offer consumers the opportunity to pay for open space and amenities as part of their house purchase. Since there is no evidence in California that consumers will buy these benefits by trading off smaller lots, they necessarily must pay in some other fashion—a longer journey to work, higher prices, smaller houses, or a combination thereof. In any case, it should be noted that whatever the consumers decide, more permanent open space within a new community means more scatteration, an evil supposedly avoided by community building.

Housing Mix

The most persistent argument for aid to, and control of, community building is that it does not provide housing for lower income families under present circumstances. It is argued that large enclaves of middle- and upper-middle-class residents are in themselves inequitable and otherwise undesirable. This was the principal reason for the program proposed in the California Housing Report. Weaver puts the case simply when he writes: "There can be, and there should be, an economic mix in the population of new communities in a democracy."

But this represents a vast oversimplification of the situation. We have already seen that the very thing buyers in new communities hope to avoid is the inclusion of lower-income families. One can recognize this without approving of it. Further, it also appears that lower-income families are improving their residential status precisely by occupying the housing left vacant by the more affluent, and that most of the housing is closer to blue-collar employment than are the new communities. There is, no doubt, some amount of subsidy which would induce lower-income families to move to new communities, and also to get higher-income residents to tolerate this. But such subsidies would certainly have to be far larger and more direct than a loan to the developer.

An increasing amount of economic separation seems more or less inevitable then. However, there are certain problems which might follow from this development that can, to an extent, be controlled. The first is the possibility that the wealthier members of society may use their spatial homogeneity to create local governments which would insulate them from contributing to the costs of the services provided for the less advantaged in the country's urban centers. However, the more taxes collected at the state and Federal levels and then returned to local governments on the basis of population and/ or need, the less meaning tax enclaves have. The country increasingly is operating in just such a manner. In California almost half the cost of primary and secondary education is borne by the state. The newly passed bill providing Federal aid to education further contributes to the trend. We shall return to this point again.

The other serious problem that stems from separation on the basis of income is that it is also likely to mean racial separation. Yet how much can be done about this through any policy of controlling or aiding privately sponsored new communities? In regard to housing policy, it seems crucially important that a single, simple principle ought to be followed wherever possible. To improve the housing of those with low incomes, one should give direct aid and let the recipients make their own choice as to where they want to live. In 1965 Congress enacted a program of rental supplements which points in this direction. Direct loans at low interest rates and grants for home ownership would also be appropriate.[8]

Most other attempts to use more devious, although perhaps politically more palatable, devices have largely failed to get assistance

to those who most needed it. Further, despite the good intentions of
the proponents of Federal aid to new communities, there is not much
chance, for the reasons already outlined, that many families with low
incomes would become residents of these developments. Once the
loans were made, the FHA would be strongly interested in the financial
security of the project. What would an administrator do when confronted with the quite plausible assertion that the market for low-priced
houses is not big enough to support a new community and that, indeed,
the few such houses that could be sold might severely decrease total
sales?

Site Planning, Design, and Innovation

Weaver, along with many other supporters of new communities,
believes that in addition to attacking the broad social questions of
public costs and the relationship of classes and races, new communities also will offer more efficient use of specific sites, more creative
design, and even outright innovation. Commenting on the possibilities
of efficient site planning, Weaver writes:

> Even if the cost of acreage increases, the price of a developed
> site to the homebuyer need not advance to the same degree.
> Indeed, good planning can produce improved lots at a lower
> cost to the home owner or renter. This has been, and can
> be, accomplished by greater clustering of dwelling units and
> inclusion of town houses and apartments on a portion of
> the available land in the development areas, so that the
> amount of land that has to be graded and improved is
> reduced. Streets and utility lines are shortened, cost
> of construction per dwelling unit is sometimes reduced
> at the same time that the number of housing units in
> the site is increased. In addition such site planning
> requires less bulldozing of trees, greater preservation
> of other scenic attributes, and wider possibilities of
> open space.[9]

Most of this argument is fallacious insofar as it implies that all
these accomplishments are more likely to come about in new communities than in an amalgamation of subdivisions. The key word in the
argument is one which has gained an almost mystical quality in the
lexicon of land development—"clustering." Clustering means the
concentration of buildings on less land than would otherwise be used.
The land that is thereby saved can be put to some public (or at least
pleasing) use—a lake, golf course, a park—or it can merely be left
untouched.

In some parts of the United States, local jurisdictions have restricted housing development to very large lots—one-half to four acres. Under such conditions, land can be better used in terms of economy, esthetics, and, ultimately, market response if houses are clustered on smaller lots (7,000 to 15,000 square feet). This is precisely what Rouse has proposed for Columbia.

Clustering can be accomplished even when ownership is fragmented. The kind of land ordinarily left unused is a mixture of hills, valley streams, rock outcroppings, etc. In other words, it is the land most difficult to develop and therefore least valuable in money terms. A county could make a master plan identifying such areas for open space and recreation, and then purchase them. The price would be nominal, especially if the land is bought before there is much surrounding development. Minimum lot sizes for the remaining land could then be reduced. The net effect would be exactly the same as clustering.

Government purchase of land for open space would raise the value of the land not purchased, but this is also what happens with a community builder. If a county felt that the benefits from such expenditures did not accrue to all its citizens, it could establish an assessment on the area affected. As residents and other land consumers took title, they would pay for the amenities, which again is what happens in a new community. The higher tax on the land, due to its increased value as well as the county's special assessment, would increase the probability of its sale for development. Holdouts might still occur, producing greater scatteration than in a new community. Since scatteration is not an unmitigated evil, this is not a serious drawback. Because land ownership usually is not concentrated, and because its assembly is extremely difficult, government should devise methods for reaching its objectives with or without single ownership.

A different kind of clustering occurs when the maximum lot is already as small as 6,000 square feet (the case in most parts of California). In this situation, land can be freed for other uses, or higher densities can be obtained, only by attaching houses. This results in what is now called the "suburban town house," referred to in the discussion of Reston. Weaver seems to be promoting such a concept when he says: "This type of land planning runs counter to the tradition of a free standing house in the 'country' surrounded by a large lot; however, where it has been well done, the consumer response has been favorable."

Of course people differ on their definition of what is "well done," but most suburban town house developments have not been favorably received by buyers. (As noted, the early evidence at Reston does not in market terms justify Simon's decision to base his whole plan on this concept.) On the other hand, it can be argued that suburban town houses offer some people a physical arrangement not otherwise

attainable and that sales will improve as time goes on. But the key
point here is that whatever the demand for the type of house now or in
the future, its development does not depend upon large scale ownership. In 1964, over 100 town-house projects were started in Orange
County, California, none of which were in a new community.

A third way to produce clustering is to build more apartments
on any given piece of land than might otherwise have been erected
and then to transfer the land saved (assuming constant over-all density)
to open space or public use. Again, there is nothing intrinsic to new
communities that would prevent this from happening elsewhere. If
a county wants a higher density of apartments, it can achieve this by
zoning regulations. It then can either purchase the unused land for
open space or require that developers hold it, as a part of a quid pro
quo for the apartments.

In predicting that new communities will bring a tide of new
creative design and innovation, its supporters are on even more
tenuous grounds. In the process of development, the community
builder necessarily becomes a land manager trying to maximize the
value of unused holdings. His essential job is to conserve, to make
sure that nothing goes on the land which will have a harmful effect in
the future. This is hardly a climate from which unusual physical forms
are likely to emerge. In fact, one may well find community builders
rejecting novel proposals of merchant builders because of the uncertain
effect they will have on the value of the land. Simon, who is trying to
make of Reston a "laboratory" for one new approach to suburban design,
is an exception, who only proves the rule.

PROBLEMS OF FEDERAL AID

New communities do offer some improvements in the physical
environment and some choices which consumers have not often had.
A new community offers a consumer the opportunity of paying either
through a longer commuting time or a higher price for a house (or
both) for parks, lakes, golf courses, and underground utilities.
Whether he makes this choice for esthetic or status or investment
reasons or to use the recreational facilities, is not relevant.

However, it is one thing to recognize a few product improvements and another to argue that public funds, through tax-exempt bonds
or direct Federal aid, should be used to aid in their creation. To
whom would the benefits of such aid flow but either to present land
owners or to the middle and upper income families who avail themselves of the opportunity to live in a new community? Thus, such aid
would represent government's commitment to confer minor benefits
upon the least needy families.

Moreover, a program of loans to community builders is fraught with paradoxes and pitfalls. In the first place, the developers most likely to apply for help are those with the least desirable and riskiest sites. An entrepreneur convinced he can do well without Federal aid is not apt to subject himself to the myriad of controls that such aid would no doubt entail. Since the state of the art of market analysis is so low and since the terms of a loan can so markedly affect the rate of return, FHA would almost be bound to set conditions to try and insure success.

Again, what would constitute an acceptable rate of return on a loan and how is it to be calculated? These are questions FHA has not had to face because in all its dealings it could rely on past market transactions. But no history of the sales of 10,000- acre holdings is available to help determine questions of market value in the case of new communities. A vicious circle would be created. The value of land and of improvements can only be determined by sophisticated investment analysis which depends on one's ability to predict the capital costs and also demand, a highly unscientific affair. If the loan is favorable enough, almost any project will succeed because it will be able to withstand high early costs and slow sales. The effect of such favorable terms would be to increase artificially the value of the land.

Still another difficulty of providing community builders with the Federal loans concerns the methods FHA would use to see that a builder's original plan is carried out. A FHA loan normally is based on a study of detailed plans and specifications, which the builder promises to follow. But is it possible or even desirable that the same method be adopted in regard to a fifteen-year project? How detailed can the plan of such a project be? To what degree can a builder adhere to it? With as much as $25 million committed to a single project, FHA in fact would have to permit changes to protect its insurance. Yet these changes might well be in conflict with the very purposes of the original program.

There is no need to go on endlessly describing the difficult decisions facing the government and the financial uncertainties involved in a program of such loans. Our case must rest on the claim that the risks are high and the potential benefits minimal.

PUBLIC SPONSORSHIP

The second part of the new-communities section of the 1965 Housing Bill is a program of low interest-rate loans to state land-development agencies. This program is designed to achieve the same results as the program of direct loans to builders, with the difference

that here the benefits of increases in land value at least would go to
the government. But in so far as the results are the same, the program in our opinion, is essentially no more valid.

There is one condition, however, under which public sponsorship
might be useful if it were made part of a program of research and
demonstration. The building and development industry does not have
firms large enough to engage in serious technological research. On
the other hand, basic science and technology probably hold much that
could be applied to make great improvements in local transportation,
communication, air temperature control, illumination, more flexible
houses, etc. The government would be spending its money wisely if
it used it to ferret out these applications and then sought to test them
in a development like a new community. Obviously, this is not the
sort of research or the sort of risks a private sponsor would be
willing to undertake.

A second kind of experimental program might involve racial
integration. Very little is known about Negro demand for housing,
but it is possible that Negroes are extremely reluctant to buy new
housing. They may fear difficulties in the buying process itself or
hostility from the other residents, and they may want to be assured
that there will be enough Negroes in the project for a reasonable
social life. (Such fears are probably strongest in working and lower
middle class Negroes.) A public or publicly funded non-profit sponsor
could be committed to maximizing opportunities in such a way that
10 to 30 percent of the residents would be Negro. The demonstration
of what it would take to make such a project viable could provide sorely
needed information on how to open up the suburbs to Negroes as they
rise financially.

It cannot be stressed too strongly that such programs should be
public efforts directed to the provision of information, not the first
step in a statewide or national program of public land ownership. They
should be part of an over-all effort at the state and Federal levels to
improve the flow of information to local agencies, public and private.

GENERAL FRAMEWORK

In none of the foregoing do we mean to imply that there are not
urgent urban problems with which the country must grapple—among
them, water and air pollution, transportation deficiencies, inadequate
housing for the poor, fiscal inequities, mal-distribution of water and
power, and mal-apportioned legislatures. That there are such problems is only too obvious. But, that the best way to alleviate them is
through "long range" physical planning if this means precise guidelines
and concommitant constraints to "achieve the plan," is very much
open to question. As political scientist Charles Lindblom has put it:

Although such an approach [long range planning] can be described, it cannot be practiced except for relatively simple problems and even then only in a somewhat modified form. It assumes intellectual capacities and sources of information that men simply do not possess and it is even more absurd as an approach to policy when the time and money that can be allocated to a policy problem is limited, as is always the case.[10]

Present urban problems can be dealt with far more effectively through changes in institutions and laws that seek to remove obstacles to equity and choice. For instance, the judicial decisions on racial segregation in public facilities (beginning with Brown vs. the Board of Education, in 1954) and on legislative apportionment (beginning with Baker vs. Carr, in 1963), are having a profound and salutary effect on the life of the country. The same will be true of the voting rights measure which Congress enacted in 1965. All these actions enable deprived citizens to have more freedom in using public facilities and in influencing their government.

The so-called Heller Plan,[11] which consists of sharing a certain portion of Federal revenues with the states, similarly addresses itself to a serious institutional problem—that the nature of our economy and our tax laws makes it very difficult for the states to raise funds commensurate with their responsibilities. The Federal government already shares its taxes through programs of grants and loans to state and local authorities. The states in turn share their revenues through general subventions and grants for specified use. Under the Heller plan, tax sharing would be increased. Further, the senior government would rebate funds, but the junior government would decide how to spend them.

Even without tax sharing, a local electorate might appropriate funds for certain needs through regional or metropolitan authorities (though in many cases the creation of such entities would involve the crossing of state lines). Two examples of such local action, by dealing with problems of transportation and pollution respectively, are the New York Port Authority and the Los Angeles Air Pollution Control District. Federal and state action to create regional governments might well constitute the removal of a further institutional barrier to constructive progress.

As mentioned earlier, the absence of large producers or consumers in the areas of housing and public facilities makes it difficult to apply basic science and technology to these concerns. The Federal government, recognizing a similar circumstance in agriculture three decades ago, undertook then an ambitious program to improve knowledge and disseminate information through direct research and agricultural extension. A Federal program of research and development to improve both the quality and quantity of schools, hospitals, transportation, libraries, and housing would be equally desirable.

Another useful program would be to give low income families greater purchasing power in the form of direct income supplements to be used for the rental or purchase of housing. Such a program would allow these families much greater latitude in deciding where to live and in what sort of housing.

The basic point of all these potential programs is that they increase the ability of private and governmental institutions to offer individuals an opportunity to make their own choices, whether with dollars or votes. This approach might be called "instrumentalism." Judicial decisions, legislative or administrative controls, subsidies, dissemination of informaton, restructuring governmental jurisdiction, and research may all improve "instruments" which help to keep a society pluralistic and open. Insofar as this is what the proponents of "planning" mean by the term, it is highly desirable. What is not desirable is "long-run" decision-making for its own sake.

Of course, there are "instrumental" actions which are bound to have effects for decades. (The San Francisco rapid transit system is one example.) In such instances, one must try to take into account all these effects while, at the same time, recognizing that predictions have a limited certainty. The aim should be always to avoid rigid determinations about life twenty years in the future. This book has criticized planning for new communities because it tried to chart such a course. It should in general be doing quite the opposite—measuring the restrictions a current act or decision may place on one's freedom to choose among alternatives at a later date. This is the approach that should underlie all public policy. Its object is not fixed forms or inaction, but programs which maximize the ability of policy makers and their constituents to choose among a set of varied courses.

The brief of this book has been with the arbitrary and purposeful preclusion of choice which seems to underlie so much of the advocacy of new towns, new communities, and other efforts to map specifically future settlement patterns. British economist Peter Self, an ardent supporter of new towns, succinctly articulates this point of view when he writes:

> The New Town approach does not deny the value of mobility, but tries to distinguish between its less and more essential aspects, and to stress that there are after all other values besides mobility and maximization of choice in jobs, homes and friends.

Maximized choice is not necessarily an optimized choice, and recognition of community values, of aesthetic patterns and of overall economic efficiency, do all in their different ways stress the point that atomistic individualism should be restrained by other perceptions.

Unlike Self, the authors believe that "optimized choice" is "maximum choice"—that what is needed from government are laws and programs which allow every individual to do, and be, what he will. There is little potential for new towns or new communities to contribute to this goal. The money and the energy which might be committed to expanding opportunity for the poor, the young, the aged, and the sick should not be diverted to real-estate ventures, no matter how noble the motives of their sponsors. Most of the people in this country who really need help—for whom the urban complex is least effective—live in the central cities. It is to these people in their present environment, primarily, that attention and money should be directed.

NOTES

1. The same proposal was rejected by Congress again in 1966.
2. Since the completion of this book, the HHFA has become the Department of Housing and Urban Development Congress enacted Title X (Housing and Urban Development Act of 1965) enabling the Department through the FHA to insure loans for land development. In 1966, Title X was expanded to embrace new communities. Insured loans under Title X have a maturity of up to seven years.
3. Robert C. Weaver, Urbanization in the Middle and Late 1960's The Lorado Taft Lecture (Evanston: University of Illinois, March 18, 1964).
4. President Johnson's message to Congress, March 12, 1965.
5. Robert O. Harvey, and W.A.V. Clark, "The Nature and Economics of Urban Sprawl," Land Economics, XLI, I (February 1965), pp. 1-9. Harvey is an economist, Clark a geographer.
6. Harvey and Clark, op cit.
7. There is a growing body of opinion questioning the supposed ill effects of sprawl. Indeed economist Jack Lessinger sees positive benefits in it: "In general we hypothesize that scatter suits an economy where growth and technological change predominate. Compaction may suit a stabilized economy, without inequalities in the distribution of income, seeking optimization of its resources." Lessinger, "The Case for Scatteration," Journal of the American Institute of Planners, XXVIII, 3 (August 1962).

8. State of California 4 percent loans to veterans are an example of such a form of direct subsidy. But such loans should be made on the basis of need rather than military service.

9. Weaver, op. cit.

10. Charles Lindblom, "The Science of Muddling Through," Public Administration Review, XIX, 2 (1959), p. 80.

11. Walter Heller, formerly Chairman of the Council of Economic Advisors to Presidents Kennedy and Johnson, made this proposal in 1964. Johnson has rejected the idea, but in 1965 several Governors strongly endorsed it.

CHAPTER

4

FEDERAL EXISTENTIALISM,
PLANNING, AND SOCIAL CHANGE:
THE OAKLAND, CALIFORNIA,
TASK FORCE

It is probably fair to say that most planners have only a vague understanding of the role the federal government has played, either purposely or by default, in meeting this nation's urban problems. Planners generally approach the "feds" as professional virgins, anxious to advertise their wares but not really anxious to commit themselves for fear of ultimate cooption (read seduction). Indeed, what linkages that do exist between most city planners and the federal government have been limited, until recently, primarily to one federal agency (the Department of Housing & Urban Development) and to a few of that agency's planning and housing programs.

This distant, somewhat tenuous relationship between a profession that lays claims to a special expertise—an expertise that is supposedly necessary if cities are to solve their major problems—and the federal government—which, since the Depression, has become more and more a partner with cities in efforts to ameliorate urban ills—may seem surprising to some. Astonishment may increase when it is realized that Uncle Sam has, through such grant programs as 701, in effect popularized, lionized, and (as we all know) subsidized the planner.

Perhaps the reason for the planner's at times ambivalent, sometimes myopic, never fully precise view of the federal establishment and his apparent inability to relate to it stems from the history of the profession. Planners were affirming through institutional

This chapter originally appeared in the Proceedings of the American Institute of Planners' Fifth Biennial Government Relations and Planning Policy Conference (Washington, D.C., 1969, American Institute of Planners), pp. 21-29.

arrangements their acceptance of logical positivism as a philosophy, political separatism as a way of life, and physical determinism as an ideology at a time when the federal government was moving in a diametrically opposite direction.

During the 1930s the social welfare function was left almost entirely to Washington. The need to rescue the nation from the Depression elevated urban economics from a subject to be debated in the classroom to a series of discreet national policy issues. Environmental concerns, when relevant, became inextricably linked to social and economic priorities. Politicians became technicians, and technicians, politicians. Resource allocation, the setting of objectives, and the development of programs reflected class and caste determinations, related political considerations, as well as the logic and rationale of the professional. Simplistic motives like "the general will" and "the public interest," were either used as convenient myths to gain consensus or submerged beneath the reality of American pluralism. Similarly the early planner's notion that good physical environments make good people was lost in a mass of contradictory evidence. When accepted by the professional as a normative frame of reference, it was generally used to provide supportive justification for acceptance of nonsensitive positions in local city government.

This harsh indictment of the planning profession is not unjust when one considers its rather peripheral contribution to meeting the problems faced by residents of urban areas. Most efforts of planners have been of little use to urban decision makers (federal, state, or local). Indeed some have apparently led to a redistribution of resources away from the poor to the more affluent members of society.

The planner's continued acceptance of the general plan as a basic tool is perhaps the source of his difficulty in becoming relevant. General or global plans are, by definition (and by necessity), long range in nature and comprehensive in scope. And despite the claims of a few, planners do not yet have, and perhaps never will have, the capacity to predict, project, and/or control accurately basic activity patterns at the city level. Attempts to do comprehensive planning, when comprehensive means all inclusive, have usually resulted in a low level of analysis and ultimately merely an aggregation of functional area plans, for housing or transportation. Conversely, if comprehensive planning is defined as meaning the planned development of linkages between and among interrelated functional areas and the time horizons remain long range, the planner's products more often than not resemble more an intellectual abstraction than an exercise in reality.

Technical deficiencies aside, the planner's retention of the irrelevant should perhaps be excused on the ground that the general plan is a legacy become conventional wisdom. Pardon is made difficult, however, when one realizes that the general plan and the general planning process appear at times to hurt those in the nation's cities who deserve least to be hurt—the poor. Comprehensive long range goals and objectives can only be developed and agreed upon by competing urban interests if the goal and objective statements are reduced to the lowest common denominator. Thus, most of our plans for the year 2000 read like petitions for God and motherhood, both white and affluent. The formula is the same almost everywhere: Mix a little bit of amenity, a dash of open space, and some new housing units; tie them together with rapid transit, lots of color, and data; be bold and even plan a new town; forget that there are real problems in today's urban areas—of resource allocation, of caste, and of class.

The general plan is most certainly a consensus tool—and the consensus heretofore in most cities has left out the disadvantaged. This circumstance has not, however, always been by choice of local decision makers. Indeed, more often than not the poor are too busy thinking of survival today to think of increased livability tomorrow. Rather than the reality of conflict and competing interests, the general plan, then, articulates a single corporate or utilitarian view of the city. Rather than priorities among functions, projects, and groups, the general plan deals with abstractions, complete rationality, comprehensivity, and equality.

The history of the planning profession as well as the profession's continued adherence to the general plan obviates an easy working relationship with the federal government. And this fact compounds the professional planner's weakness in coping with urban realities—particularly the realities of poverty, discrimination, and alienation in urban America.

To get back in the game will not be easy for the planner. One of the first steps for him to take, however, should be to develop an understanding of the federal delivery system and decision-making process. Indeed, understanding this system and this process will, because of some real, direct analogies, provide him with real insight into the basic pluralism of interests and groups in urban areas and the resulting complexities of "the urban problem," assuming the solution of the problem is at all related to resource allocation.

THE ORIGIN OF THE OAKLAND TASK FORCE

Since 1960 nearly 100 new programs directly affecting the quality of urban life have been enacted by the Congress. Additionally two new departments and one addition to the Office of the President have been created and granted defined responsibilities to assist in meeting urban needs. Despite recognition in law and structure of

the urban crisis and the broad array of programs to meet this crisis,
qualitative as well as quantitative indexes testify that the situation
remains bleak.

Oakland, California, is probably no better or worse off than
most large urban areas. All the "normal" statistical indexes of
environmental, group, and personal poverty have been and continue
to be recorded for it. Federal involvement in Oakland appears to
differ only in degree from similar involvement in municipalities of
similar size with a similar litany of problems.

Recent efforts at calculating the number of individual federal
programs now being used in Oakland vary considerably, depending
on the researcher's definition of program. What is clear, however (no
matter who the calculator is), is that a lot of federal money is going
into the city by various routes, to various groups, public and private.

The knowledge that Oakland, California, was the beneficiary
of a variety of federally funded programs and that neither federal nor
city administrators had an appropriate coordinative handle on the
funds led to the creation of the Oakland Task Force by the San Francisco
Federal Executive Board (FEB). It also engendered support of the
Task Force by high level regional and Washington federal administrators.

Three interrelated assumptions provided the rationale and
frame of reference of the Task Force:

1. Coordination among Federal programs and agencies involved
in Oakland and, by implication, most other cities, was at best minimal,
and at worst nonexistent.

2. Similarly and quite related, a common federal strategy for
dealing with Oakland's many problems was more a dream than a
reality.

3. Lack of coordination and lack of common strategy resulted
in a less than optimum achievement level for federal programs in
Oakland.

An early working paper presented to the Task Force commented
on those assumptions:

> Development of a viable federal role in Oakland has been
> made difficult because of the multiplicity of federal pro-
> grams and the disparate objectives as well as adminis-
> trative processes associated with their use . . . .
> The pluralism reflected in the number and type of
> federal "aids" is mirrored in the institutional arrange-
> ments in Washington and the field for implementing
> them . . . . The net effect has been to minimize the
> leverage the Feds have to affect solution of urban prob-
> lems . . . . The effectiveness and creditability of the

federal local partnership has been weakened. More important, significant opportunities to improve the quality of life of urban areas have been lost.

Thus the absence of and the need for a coordinated response and common strategy governed the development of the Task Force structure as well as its work program.

THE STRUCTURE OF THE OAKLAND TASK FORCE

Because the FEB, both nationally and locally, does not have separate funding sources, monies to operate the Task Force were secured from five arms of the federal government: the Department of Housing and Urban Development (HUD); the Department of Health, Education, and Welfare (HEW); the Office of Economic Opportunity (OEO); the Department of Labor (DOL); and the Department of Commerce (DOC). This was in and of itself no mean achievement, as anyone familiar with efforts to procure funds for single projects from two or more federal departments must know. Only through the patient prodding of Robert Weaver of HUD and the general commitment to the Task Force on the part of many of the under and assistant secretaries, particularly Robert Wood (HUD) and Ross Davis (DOC), was sufficient capital finally secured to initiate the work program.*

Once funds were available, the Task Force became a viable entity, for which Robert Pitts, the regional administrator of HUD, provided an initial and sustained leadership. Charles Patterson, special assistant to the assistant secretary of the Economic Development Administration (EDA), was selected as chairman of the Task Force. Local staff was provided by the author's firm (Marshall Kaplan, Gans, and Kahn), the author serving as technical director. Each contributing federal agency assigned a senior staff member to the Task Force, who was, ostensibly, to allocate a substantial amount of time to the Task Force. The collective assignments of the departments and OEO were to provide a working staff, which would leave "agency hats" behind while serving on the Task Force.

Both the projected time commitments and the sought-for independence of Task Force members were only partially achieved during

---

*Each agency was asked to contribute $25,000. Funds from four were made available at the outset, while the initially recalcitrant fifth made amends midway through the project. EDA served as the funding agent.

implementation of the work program. This was understandable in that
most assignees had dual and at times triple responsibilities. Further,
in that the Task Force was involved in a critique of the federal delivery system and decision-making process—a critique that at times
rubbed raw the sensitive nerves of many individual agencies—Task
Force members were at times very conscious of their pedigrees and
felt a need to get their own agencies' reviews of analyses and findings.

Surprisingly, despite these problems, Task Force members
did function effectively. My firm's staff of necessity provided the
working force, leaving the federal personnel to serve in effect as a
board of directors. While at various times, individual "board members" did feel it necessary to secure departmental sign-offs, these
sign-offs did not appear in most instances to dilute content. Indeed,
because the results of the Task Force's efforts reflected by and
large an inside critique and because sign-off was secured from each
participating Task Force member as well as his agency, commitment
to implementation was and remains strong.

THE WORK PROGRAM AND FINDINGS

The basic work program of the Task Force was divided into
three components: (1) to define with a counterpart city/county Task
Force Oakland's problems and the federal response to these problems;
(2) to analyze the federal decision-making process and its impact; and
(3) to recommend steps to make the federal delivery system more
effective in meeting Oakland's needs and priorities. The results of
each component are summarized below.

Oakland's Problems and the Federal Response

Despite the fact that Oakland had been the recipient of many
federal planning grants (environmental, social, and economic), the
city Task Force was not easily able to define its problems, nor was
it able, except in a very general nonprogrammatic manner, to identify
priorities among and between problems. In turn, while the city/county
Task Force and the federal Task Force were able finally to achieve
consensus statements about what the city's problems were in the
environmental and economic areas of concern, they were unable to
do so in the social areas of concern.

Oakland is not unlike most other cities in this nation when it
comes to problem and priority definition. To date, planners for the
reasons indicated earlier, have been of little use to chief executives
in this regard. Unable to provide tough day-to-day problem and

priority analysis, they have sought refuge in the long range planning
process and plan. Neither process nor plan provides a viable tool
to negotiate conflicting local interests or to rate problems and priorities ordinally or cardinally, particularly when allocation questions
are involved.

Oakland is structured neither politically nor institutionally in
such a way as to permit ready city hall definition of problems. For
example, independent and semiindependent departments exist, each
having its own set of often competing interests. Further, city hall
as a collective entity is viewed with suspicion bordering on hostility
by many of the city's poor (primarily black and brown) population
(more than 33 percent of city residents). Communication and dialogue
takes place most often in an atmosphere of confrontation.

In many respects the federal role to date has both reflected
and strengthened the institutional and group pluralism evident in Oakland. Federal programs are funded directly to many public and private groups by various federal agencies, each conscious and protective of its own client and constituent groups and each committed
to its own set of often highly particularized objectives. Indeed,
primarily because of the varied routing systems used by most federal
agencies in Oakland, the differences in program funding cycles and
method of disbursement, the Task Force, while able to prepare a comprehensive inventory of federal efforts in Oakland, was not able to
record a complete inventory, even after a three-month effort.

The Federal Decision-Making Process and Impact

The analysis of the federal decision-making process and the
impact of this process on Oakland is probably the phase of the work
program that is of most national significance. It was this phase of
the study that defined the many impediments to interagency and intraagency coordination and development of common strategy. It was
also this phase of the study that suggested to the Task Force the need
to define precisely the meaning of coordination, particularly as it
relates to issues of strategy and planning and ultimately to federal-
city relationships. Definitions finally arrived at led the Task Force
to assume a different position concerning the meaning and impact
of coordination than it had at the outset of the work program. The
following findings of the Task Force pertaining to the federal
decision-making process were arrived at—neither completely presented here nor scaled in importance, for purposes of brevity.

The Federal Regional Organization

Only in three federal agencies do the regional offices have direct control and supervision of their respective organizational components. These three are HUD, OEO, and the Small Business Administration. HEW's regional office has what might be called persuasive powers, while the Department of Transportation and the Department of Agriculture have no regional office control over regional line agencies. DOL's regional organization reflects hybrid tendencies. That is, its Manpower Administration has direct control over BWTP but only persuasive powers over most other DOL components. EDA's Oakland project is unique to that agency in that it is limited to that city and the administrators of the project report directly to Washington.

The Processing of Federal Programs

Significant and basic differences were found in processing procedures and requirements among federal programs. Supposedly complementary federal programs in different agencies and even in the same agency are processed differently. Little uniformity exists in regard to timing, number of events associated with routing systems, the various sign-offs required, and the time allocated for regional and/or Washington review. Even within the same program authorization, processing procedures for individual projects vary widely, depending on priorities, the number of applications in the pipeline, the number of offices involved in the review and approval sequence, and so forth.

Statutory and Administrative Guidelines

The Task Force compared the objectives and provisions of the legislation governing fourteen prototypical federal programs with the guidelines developed by federal departments to administer the same programs. Analysis revealed that (1) certain provisions in the statutes inhibit maximum effectiveness, or even use, of a given program and may hinder realization of Congress's stated objectives; (2) administrative guidelines, in the manner they define the intent of Congress, program eligibility, funding and program requirements, and review and approval processes may limit the reach or dilute the purposes of the statute; and (3) wide inconsistencies between and among and internal to supposedly complementary criteria concerning objectives, eligibility requirements, funding patterns, application and processing procedures, provisions for coordination, and location of decision-making authority seriously impede development of coordinative processes and products. Where provisions for coordination are included, they tend to be vague, general, and suggestive, rather than mandatory.

Perception of Roles: Senior Regional Federal Officials

Intensive interviews were held with senior staff members of every federal agency having significant program involvement in Oakland. These interviews indicate that (1) there is little consensus among different agencies about the major problems facing the city; (2) agency officials tend to define Oakland's problems in terms of their own agencies' areas of concern; (3) wide differences in perspective exist in regard to individual agency missions and roles in Oakland—even internal to the same agency; and (4) different perceptions exist in certain agencies about organization, structure, and program responsibility.

None of the officials interviewed could give an operative definition of coordination or indicate how coordinative processes might be meaningfully implemented. Except in relatively few cases, none of those interviewed appeared significantly concerned about the apparent lack of interagency and even intraagency coordination.

The Impact of Federal Programs

Lack of a complete inventory of federal programs in Oakland combined with the fact that some agencies recorded only obligations and not disbursements denied the Task Force the opportunity to develop an economic model capable of testing the aggregate impact of federal funds. As an alternative, a model was created and successfully used to evaluate the short term effect of selected federal grant and loan programs. The results indicated that "software" programs (social services) have a much greater short term impact on jobs and the local tax base than do "hardware" programs (capital facilities), because of (1) the direct transfer payments associated with most software programs and (2) the amount of financial transactions involved in hardware programs.

Case Studies

The major findings of the Task Force concerning the federal delivery system outlined above were illustrated clearly in two case studies prepared by the group. These case studies covered the Concentrated Employment Program and the Neighborhood Center Pilot Program. Both programs were conceived of as efforts at meshing together several federal programs to achieve specific objectives, and both had achieved tangible beginnings in Oakland at the time of the studies, the former being in its second year and the latter being about ready to be implemented in three-dimensional form. Problems had beset both efforts however, partly because of (1) the lack of clarity about role and resource contributions; (2) the lack of clarity about decision-making power; (3) communication gaps between federal agencies in Washington and their counterparts in the region; (4) differences in outlook and objectives among federal agencies; and (5) difficulties in securing funds for supposedly complementary parts of each program.

Definitions and Recommendations

It is to the Task Force's credit that it resisted the urge to strive for neatness and simplicity in its recommendations. Faced with a federal system that was, and remains, existential in character, the Task Force would have been excused if it had merely repeated many of the shibboleths of the past and opted for a more structured, centrally directed decision-making process. Instead it faced up to the task of redefining the meaning of coordination and strategy within the federal context.

Three decision-making models were seen in evidence at the federal level in Oakland. These were defined as central direction, mutual interaction, and adaptation. Each model is different, as the outline indicates.[1]

Type	Prerequisites	Type of Planning	Coordinative Process
Central Direction	Shared defined common purposes	Efforts at overall departmental planning; synoptic long- as well as short-range planning	Mandate of order
Mutual Interaction	Some shared defined purposes; mutual understanding as to general inter- and intradepartmental objectives	Functional planning, short- and long-	Sharing of information; persuasive dialogue; playing by the rules of the game
Adaptation	Minimial shared defined purposes; some competing purposes; minimal knowledge of other departments' or agencies' purposes.	Ad hoc, short-range	Negotiation, bargaining, chance

Implicit in the outline are many different meanings of the term
coordination. Many of these meanings are consistent with one another;
others are quite inconsistent. For example, coordination has been
defined at times primarily in terms of the process of decision making
rather than the results of that decision making.[2] In this regard,
central direction is regarded as a process in many coordinative systems[3] while mutual interaction[4] and/or adaptation is inherent in others.
The need for common and shared objectives is a requirement for
coordination, according to some in the federal government, while only
acceptance of rules of behavior is a prerequisite for others. A very
few examples of "coordinative efforts" suggest that neither agreed-
upon purposes nor consensus about the rules of behavior is essential.
Rather, coordination results from an adaptation of specific decisions
or decision makers to other decisions or decision makers.[5] Various
processes to secure this adaptation become visible, including negotiation, bargaining, compromise, and so forth. In terms of results,
coordination has been limited in definition by spatial boundaries,[6] by
clients or beneficiaries,[7] and by assigned functional areas of concern.[8]

The case for coordination is often stated negatively; that is,
it is seen as a process of avoiding strategies and programs that are
inconsistent. Consistency and harmony, however, does not necessarily
require conscious efforts on the part of decision makers. These
qualities could accrue to processes and products by chance or by a
response on the part of one decision maker to an action of another
without their ever conversing or meeting.

Only when the term strategy is used with coordination is there
any clear mandate for a conscious and/or purposeful effort at achieving
coordination. In this instance an assumption is made that the results
of a common strategy and a coordinative process will be more satis-
factory to one or more of the decision makers than an individual action
taken later by one of them, without a common strategy and a coordinative process.

That common strategies and coordinative processes and products are not common results from the fact that the present federal
system clearly reflects the basic pluralistic nature of American
society. Different constituencies and client groups generally fasten
themselves onto particular programs and particular departments,
often prior to their final formulation. Indeed, the public interest
reveals itself often to be an aggregation of competing individual and
group interests.

Pejorative judgments should not be made casually about the
federal system. Its accomplishments are many. Further, only those
few whose conceit permits them to dare pose a global solution to our
urban ills could feel confident about substituting a more directive
system of decision making for the present one. In many respects,

the public market place of federal programs permits us to make
mistakes, to experiment, and to move ahead incrementally, when
knowledge permits, in selected functional areas.

The Task Force rejected central direction as a structural
principal governing action between agencies—central direction as a
coordinative system being based on the premise that some one person
or group of persons has an overall understanding of the ramifications
of each decision and an overall ability to foresee the benefits and
costs of each decision. Because different perceptions of problems
and solutions exist among most agencies with functional missions and
because no one really knows the answers with respect to Oakland's
problems, central direction is rarely used to program and implement
interagency coordinative efforts, apparently because the risk of in-
curring social, economic, and physical costs far outweighs any benefits.
Central direction, according to the Task Force, is a valuable organiz-
ing principal only when missions, objectives, and functions are clearly
defined and hard data are available for making measurable judgments
about benefits and costs and, perhaps, when federal agencies are
responding to locally approved plans and programs. Both these instances suggest central direction as a coordinative device primarily
in functional areas and within specific departments. Mutual interaction and/or adaptation appear the two most relevant coordinative
processes with respect to interdepartmental coordination.

Once the frame of reference outlined above was accepted, the
orientation of Task Force recommendations became clear. Rather
than define basic structural changes, they deal primarily with process
amendments. The basic objective of the Task Force was to create
conditions increasing options open for departments to develop common
strategies and coordinative processes and products if they desired to.
That is, the objective was to eliminate present impediments to coordinative options.

Task Force proposals cover six broad areas:

1. The need to grant regional offices of federal agencies direct
supervision over their departments and review and approval processes
over grant and loan programs.

2. The need to create a permanent interagency group composed
of regional administrators in each region.

3. The need to clarify and define departmental missions and
functional areas of concern.

4. The need to simplify and amend present application routing
systems or review processes.

5. The need to develop local uniform information systems
relative to federal investment.

6. The need to develop and increase the administrative, planning,
and managerial capacity of local chief executives.

CONCLUSIONS

The analysis of how the federal system functions in Oakland
could be repeated with the same results in city after city. The basic
determinant of the system, the pluralism inherent in American society,
is generic. Indeed, only because the federal government assumed
the social welfare function in urban areas during the Depression did
this pluralism become masked by a corporate view of urban life and
the myth of the public interest. In essence, both the War on Poverty
and the Model Cities program have realized this and concentrated
on the problems of the least fortunate in our society.

The Federal system suggests many options for planners willing
to commit themselves to playing the resource allocation game on the
side of the disadvantaged. Inside the system the planner can legitimately
serve as an advocate of a constituency—the urban and rural poor.
The openness of the system—the many leverage points in it—permit
the planner to function in many roles. These range from having an
impact on the development of administrative criteria to the actual
management and operation of programs. That these roles are important can be seen in the historical development of HUD's Model
Cities Administration (MCA) and OEO. In both instances, inside
advocates were responsible for affecting major departmental policy
decisions relative to citizen participation processes, program
planning requirements, and program funding determinations, and
many other program elements. If government is seen as an agent of
social and institutional change, then first OEO and now apparently
HUD's MCA must be granted high marks as change agents and inside
advocates high marks as catalysts in the process of change.

Outside the federal system the planner acting inside city hall
as advocate for the poor can serve, if he understands the process,
to link federal and local resources to the problems of the poor.
Borrowing on the rationale generating creation of such incremental
neighborhood, class, and caste oriented planning programs as the
War on Poverty and the Model Cities program, and the lessons learned
from each, the planner can begin to reflect further on the weaknesses
inherent in the array of technical tools now open to him. Alternatives
to present planning approaches are available that would clearly define
local planning processes in short term, functional limited area,
direct resource allocation terms—terms more real and vital than
present planning processes. Increased involvement in and extension
of the Model Cities program concept would be one productive area of
concern—one with potentially high payoffs to the professional and to
his new constituency—the urban poor.

Finally, perhaps the most difficult role for the planner to assume is that of advocate to ghetto groups. As an advocate planner the professional faces many problems as well as opportunities. It is not easy, particularly if one is white, to work in a black ghetto. Alternative courses of action are not always clear and benefit-cost equations are difficult to achieve. Knowledge of the range of federal programs, while not the only asset needed, would certainly assist the planner in helping local groups translate needs into reality.

In conclusion, planners face a crisis of relevance. Such issues as the meaning of coordination and common strategy, which were examined by the Oakland Task Force with respect to the federal system, need reexamination by planners in local communities throughout the nation. Indeed, these terms are often used to describe characteristic elements of planning processes and plans. Their significance, without precise and limited definitions in terms of achieving social change, is questionable.

But many options are open to the planner, including the following:

1. Redirection of existing planning processes away from a long range, areawide planning framework to an incremental, area-bounded, functionally oriented framework.

2. Insertion of social as well as economic priorities into planning processes—in effect perceiving of planning as purely a resource allocation tool

3. Reorganization of local planning departments on a horizontal basis and provision of planners for many of the existing line departments

4. Provision of a central staff to mayors and/or city managers (federal aid) to help determine priorities among competing public and private groups.

5. Provision of professional assistance to local community groups (federal aid).

NOTES

1. Charles E. Lindblom, The Intelligence of Democracy (New York: The Free Press, 1966), p. 168. Lindblom's book provides many excellent insights concerning alternative definitions of coordination. These insights, although amended by the Oakland experience, assisted the Task Force in defining coordination models.

2. FEB represents an example of a coordinative decision-making process. The institution is not, in Oakland or any other cities, directed primarily at a product.

3. HUD's organization in the region, as it affects Oakland, illustrates central direction over constituent offices.

4. HEW's organization, in turn, reflects coordination through mutual interaction instead of central direction.

5. A good example of this is OEO's and DOL's relationship in the Concentrated Employment Program (CEP).

6. The Model Cities program illustrates a coordinated effort limited, by definition, by spatial boundaries.

7. The War on Poverty, although defined by target areas, is primarily directed at a set of specific clients, the urban poor.

8. The CEP effort portrays coordination in a specific functional area.

THE PLANNING PROFESSION:
A NEW SET OF GROUNDRULES

In each chapter of Part II commentary is offered on alternate roles planners can assume if they desire to play a relevant part in helping the nation shape effective urban policies and solve urban problems. Taken together, all the chapters provide a new set of norms for the planner. These norms clearly reject the need (1) for the planner to separate his value system from his professional agenda; (2) for the planner to focus primarily on the physical environment because of its supposed primacy in improving human conditions; and (3) for the planner to avoid "contaminating" his work by involvement in politics.

Chapter 5, "Advocacy and Urban Planning", describes some of the author's experiences as an advocate planner. It illustrates the marginal benefits of advocacy planning, given the political economy of scarcity we live in. Conversely, it suggests that advocacy planning is quite consistent with pluralism inherent in our cities and the tenuous nature of the planner's knowledge about what works and what does not work. Apart from providing various groups—particularly the poor—with a better shake in terms of resource allocation, advocacy planning may serve to limit the harm resulting from the historic failure to involve effectively the many publics likely to be affected by plans in the planning process.

Just prior to the passage of the Model Cities legislation, the author was asked by the AIP to participate in a symposium on model cities. This invitation resulted in the brief paper on the Demonstration Cities program which appears as Chapter 6. It reflects the author's hope at that time the Model Cities program would stimulate a new kind of planner. More precisely it reflects the author's interpretation of the Model Cities legislation, and accompanying administrative criteria as a mandate to city planners to grant primacy to social and economic priorities; to the needs and priorities of the poor; to the immediate present rather than to the long distant future; to limited geographic areas rather than the whole cities; to specific functional problems rather than the totality of problems related to human existence.

Chapter 7, "The Roles of the Planner and the Developer in the New Community" presents a critique of the role planners have played in the development of new towns policy and programs, relating it to a prescription for what that role should be. That prescription suggests that, consistent with his role in built-up areas, the new town planner should concern himself more with defining the different and varying

spatial needs of specific and different groups of people than with defining the overall form and shape of the new town environment. More
important, as for cities, the planner of new towns should be less
concerned with defining a plan for the year 2000 than with defining
who gets benefits proposed in short-term public or private plans.
Equal treatment in terms of time and expenditures is not available to
all groups and areas of the urban complex. And certainly, the efforts
of planners should be directed, at least in part, toward increasing the
probability that more economic, social, and environmental options
are open to the least advantaged members of society.

Chapter 8 contains the author's presentation before the 1970 Conference of Mayors entitled "Random thoughts on Planning, Problems
and Approaches: Small Cities." It provides some precise guidelines
concerning the close relationship needed between planner and city hall.
Further, decrying the reliance of many cities on consultants and
reviewing the negative impact of consultants, it proposes alternatives
relative to building up staff capacity. Finally, this chapter makes a
plea for more rather than less resident involvement in planning and
less rather than more emphasis on long range, comprehensive planning. In this regard, it suggests that areas of maximum opportunity
rather than the whole city or the whole range of human conditions
and problems be selected by the planner for his attention.

Chapter 9 presents an analysis of the relationship between the
model cities program and national urban policy, and Chapter 10 relates
human problems to ways of solving them. Both chapters project—
and view with equanimity—the increasing politicization of the planning
process. Both imply that the next wave, or generation, of urban programs will contain less detailed administrative criteria and involve
less categorization than the programs that now exist. If this projection
is accurate, it will be necessary for local officials to become more
acutely aware of the impact of decisions on the allocation of scarce
resources among and between different groups. And it will be necessary
for the planner, if he is to be relevant, to risk participation in a
clarification of the impact of specific allocation alternatives on specific groups. It will be increasingly necessary for the planner to be
prepared to advocate particular courses of action—action affecting
particular groups and people. Professional life will not be easy for
the planner, but it may be more meaningful.

5

To date, the city planning profession and, therefore, most city planners have played a peripheral role in American urban life. Steeped in a philosophical tradition of logical positivism, planners have for the most part viewed their role as primarily that of applying the value system of others to a set of facts which they can aggregate, analyze, and (under guidance) forge into a set of alternative programs and strategies. This bifurcation of fact and value parallels the historical fears of the planning profession to "mix in politics." Indeed, one of the earliest institutions to evolve from the acceptance of planning as a city function was the planning commission. Its prime function, besides serving as collective salesman for the still embryonic profession, was to separate the planner from the "evil" influences of city hall.

The separation by fiat reflected in the insertion of the commission between technician and politician merely ratified the already accepted normative behavior pattern that technicians should, like mystics, receive values from the outside. Both the institution and the philosophy would have been enough to lessen the impact of the emerging profession. Unfortunately, however, a third millstone was added as a burden. In essence, city planning and the city planner were mesmerized by their concern, primarily with the physical environment, and their acceptance of a deterministic view of the importance of that environment. Paraphrasing Robert Frost, good neighborhoods make good people.

This chapter originally appeared in The Social Welfare Forum (New York: Columbia University Press, 1968, published for the National Conference on Social Welfare), pp. 58-77.

Unfortunately, planning came of age during an aseptic era in American city government. In effect, the combined influence of the New Deal and the local government reformer diminished the role of city hall as a broker of conflict, as a place where often-times competing individual, group, and community interests could be resolved with a level of acrimony tolerable to all but the most sensitive white patrician. The New Deal, in elevating and formalizing the resource-allocation game, bypassed local government for the most part, and weakened the influence of the local politician. Similarly, the end of partisan local primaries, the termination of the ward system, the use of at-large municipal elections,[1] the increased number of independent commissions in many large cities, and the coming of age of the city manager system helped convert the role of the politician from that of broker to that of administrator.

The evolution of local governmental structure and process represented a victory of sorts for the new American middle class. Politics and poker were synonymous with the ethics of the "potato eater," the "kike," and the "wop." The "spade" and the "spic" had not yet achieved political visibility. Conversely, the "honest, impartial, and efficient pursuit of the interests of the community as a whole" was indicative of the emerging ethics of a white, middle-class, Protestant society. Indeed, as the American dream became converted into reality[2] for an increasingly large number of Americans, the immigrant became Protestantized, accepted the ethic and opted for a clean political system.

To the planner, this evolution in city government conformed to his predefined and accepted behavior pattern. Positivism became institutionalized by the ingathering of technicians at city hall, politics became sanitized by the city manager and civil service systems, and physical determinism became emphasized in the concern for making cities beautiful, efficient, and economical. Uncle Sam reduced the need for the city to be occupied with social welfare.

The primary tool of the planner, the general plan, was the complete image of the evolution. Rather than conflict and competing interests as a way of urban life, the general plan reflected consensus, and pejorative acceptance of a corporate or utilitarian view of the city. Rather than recognize class and/or caste, the general plan usually perceived only infrastructure and enveloping land use. Rather than assuming priorities among and between functions and projects, priorities based on the strength of competing claims of competing groups, the general plan assumed complete rationality, comprehensibility, and an equality "possible" as an abstraction but denied in the real world.

Although such an approach can be described, it cannot be practiced except for relatively simple problems and even then only in a somewhat modified form. It assumes intellectual capacities and sources of information that men simply do not possess, and it is even more absurd as an approach to policy when the time and money that can be allocated to a policy problem is limited, as is always the case.[3]

For the most part, city planning and city planners have had only minimal impact on the decision-making processes. Originally, this lack of impact was blamed by the professional on the system. Academic tomes, as well as speeches at annual conventions of the American Institute of Planners, emphasized the fact that, while truth, beauty, and wisdom had been captured and internalized by the profession, "them outsiders" would not listen. Mayors, councilmen, and even city managers had somehow mistakenly neglected to follow the planners' essentially normative planning process and product, while their constituents often cruelly rejected or, worse, closed their ears to the planners' conventional wisdom about the physical environment.

Only recently has the profession turned inward, and turned introspective. The plain facts of life appear to be that long-range, multifunctional tools like the general plan are quite irrelevant to urban life. Because consensus can often be achieved in present-day, urban America by reducing goals or objectives to their lowest common denominator, most plans read like admonitions to God and Motherhood and, in most cases, God and Mother are white. Where a precise statement, either in the form of objective or proposal, is made, the long-range nature of that statement emphasizes its Alice-in-Wonderland quality and weakens its impact or import. The comprehensiveness sought of the planner is denied by both intellectual limitations and the impossibility of the task itself.

Perhaps our inability and ineffectiveness in striving for the comprehensive have led to our need to be specific and precise about such mandated responsibilities as zoning and subdivision regulations, urban renewal, and capital improvement programs. Here again, our record has not been too successful. Here again, our response has been first to blame those bad guys on the outside. Market pressures personalized as those "evil speculators and land developers" have wreaked havoc on land-use controls and assisted in making urban renewal a perversion of objectives, while pressures of competing groups often reduce sheltered capital improvement programs and capital budgets to a shambles. Where these tools have had an impact, this impact has often been inimical to the interests of the least favored group—the

urban poor. Indeed, with proper funding and a sabbatical from current
pursuits, it would not be too difficult to prove that plans and planners
have served through engagement in the planning process to redistribute
local resources away from the have-nots to the haves.

Positivism, physical determinism, and political separation do
not provide the planner with a working set of premises or guidelines
commensurate with the realities of urban life. The advent of the war
on poverty, now followed by the model cities program, indicates a
changing set of national priorities and perspectives. Both offer opportunities to redefine the urban planning function and process.

Not only did the original Office of Economic Opportunity (OEO)
mandate recognize the "hidden" poverty in our central cities, it also
recognized that community interests may not equate with group
interests. The phrase "maximum feasible participation" of the poor
was purposely utilized, to the surprise of most congressmen and most
mayors as well as of most early progenitors of the war, to build up in
communities throughout the land countervailing structures within
which the poor (or their supposed representatives) could compete for
limited public and private goods and services. In many cases this
"advocacy" took place within city hall (as in Oakland), while in others
it took place outside city hall (as in San Francisco). The choice, however, was not one for local officialdom to make entirely independently,
for up to 1967 it was not necessary for OEO's resource stream to
pass through city hall.

The Department of Housing and Urban Development (HUD), in
administering the model cities program, follows a more institutionalized route than OEO. The program is clearly directed at and
through city halls. While citizen participation is mandated, its form
and substance are left for local definition—a definition which must
be approved by local governmental entities.

Despite their differences, the war on poverty and the model cities
program contain, implicit in their framework, a welcome definition
of local government different from that subscribed to by historical
addicts of governmental reform and a planning process quite contrary
to that practiced by most professionals.

Both programs view one of the prime functions of city government
as resource distribution and direction. Both programs favor a local
political system where political dialogue concerning resource allocation
is a way of life and incremental decision-making a process and a
product. Rather than utilitarian objectives, the war on poverty and
the model cities program suggest specific class and/or caste objectives
and seek from local government a recognition of these objectives.

Decision-making concerning resource allocation, whether public
and/or private, is premised in both programs as a result of constantly competing (and shifting) interests and constantly competing

(and shifting) objectives. Both attempt to present a frame of reference, a set of conditions where competing objectives and interests can be debated and resolved through the process of adaptation, compromise, negotiation, and even contention. Both recognize the historical weaknesses of the poor in playing the resource-allocation game and both consciously attempt through fiat and process to redress this balance and assure for them an improved delivery system and some involvement in deciding the content of, and control over, that system.

The war on poverty and the model cities program define planning in resource-allocation terms. Concern for the micro environment of specific neighborhoods, specific blocks, and specific people takes precedence over concern for all neighborhoods, all blocks, and all people. Systemic, rational, and comprehensive planning is considered, correctly, to be impossible to achieve and is replaced by a more incremental, functional process and product, one that chooses the certainty of immediate predictable results rather than a long-term, speculative impact. Finally, rather than plan for, the planner is asked to plan with, the recipients of his technical beneficence; rather than separate fact and value, the planner is asked to join the two.

ADVOCACY

Implementation of the war on poverty and the model cities program has resulted in a debate in the planning profession concerning advocacy. The term "advocate" has recently been used for the professional planner whose clients are the havenots in our society. Unfortunately, neither the term nor the role it implies has ever been described in a precise manner. Therefore, it has meant all things to all people. Its shrill connotations have sent undue fear into the hearts of federal as well as local officials (particularly redevelopment directors). One well-known and well-qualified redevelopment official, after challenging the need for two sets of project planners—one to serve a community group and one from his own agency—saw the advocate as the curse of mankind, or at least of his own agency—"all you social planners who get in the way of progess."

Self-chosen (or anointed) advocates often view themselves, mistakenly, more as generals in a singular war against an often-undefined establishment. Neither the perspective of the fearsome official who often must compute success in terms of units produced rather than people benefited and must meet project deadlines nor that of the ideologically oriented, anti-establishment technician should prevail in charting this new avenue of endeavor for professionals. The term "advocate" has been borrowed from the law. Therefore, we should look there for our definition of role and process. The advocate in the legal profession is responsible for defending or prosecuting. In addition, he may "broker" the system for clients; that is, he advises them in regard to the relationship between the law and their objectives and programs and, at times, pleads these objectives. Ultimate arbiters exist in the form of judges, juries, and/or quasi-judicial commissions, and so forth. Advocates for contending parties join issues when "facts" are interpreted differently or when the body of law applying to these facts is interpreted differently.

The planning advocate functions in much the same way. His role is to defend or prosecute the interests of his clients when he and they together think that they need prosecution and/or defense. Rather than linking the law to objectives, the planning advocate links resource and strategy alternatives to objectives. He joins issues at the request of his client when the facts interpreted by others overlook, minimize, and/or negatively affect his clients' interests. Like an attorney, the planning advocate has a choice of several avenues through which to advise his clients. These might include independence, coalition, negotiation, and/or contention. Hybrids and/or mutants are possible within each strategy over a given time. Unlike members of the legal profession, the planning advocate relies not on judges and juries as final arbiters, but on the communities' political system. In planning advocacy, unlike the due process of law, resolution of contention is not absolute and/or final but is usually incremental. As in the legal profession, the defined objectives, priorities, and ultimate strategy of the client must, in cases of conflict, take precedence over those of the professional so long as the professional-client relationship exists. The professional can always opt out if selected value systems and defined courses of action cause him moral or professional anguish.

THE REASON FOR ADVOCACY

The role of the planning advocate is premised on the following hypotheses:

1. The present distribution of public and/or private resources in the cities of this nation is skewed away from the have-nots to the haves. Even a cursory look at most capital improvement programs, capital budgets, bond issues, and city budgets suggests that most cities have yet to heed the imperative of the National Commission on Civil Disorders. Speaking of the need to solve the problems of this nation's ghettos, the Commission proposed: "There can be no higher priority for national action and no higher claim on the nation's conscience."[4]

2. Even when resources are directed at the poor, at the ghettos, they fail to take cognizance of expressed needs and priorities of

residents. Interviews carried out by our firm with residents in
Hunter's Point (San Francisco), Oakland (California), and Bedford-
Stuyvesant (New York) clearly indicate that, assuming a priority
equation premised on marginal-dollar concepts, most residents would:
elect "software" (social services, job training and development, education) rather than "hardware" (capital facility) programs; unlike
most public planners, treat the restructuring of the physical environment as of less import than job, income, and education issues; view
urban renewal as nothing less than the American tragedy or, more
accurately, the American blacks' tragedy; suggest nuances as to the
meaning of space and the environment rarely enunciated even by the
best architects or planners (such as preferences for small, unstruc-
tured spaces rather than larger spaces; for defined block and community structure rather than democratic opaqueness).

3. Most large urban cities have not yet derived rational priority
definition processes. Priorities and programs more often than not
suggest an adaptive and incremental decision-making process rather
than an over-all, coordinated process. Negotiation, compromise, and
contention between and among several groups and individuals in the
public and private sector create the rules of the game rather than any
synoptic and systemic design. Ghetto residents and ghetto groups
are underrepresented, both in numbers and in influence in this
decision-making process. In addition, decades of discrimination,
complemented by an often psychic distance from city hall and downtown and compounded by a personal priority system directed at
personal rather than group survival, have impeded the effectiveness,
until recently, of the poor as game players.

4. Heretofore, it has been convenient and perhaps necessary to
imagine our local decision-making process as an expression of the
community will, the public interest, and the popular consensus. The
popular vote has been accepted as sanctifying the process and recent
Supreme Court decisions as lending it a halo effect. Certainly, this
is part of our national mythology and lends rationality to public
decisions. Yet, if we are to understand the situation, it is necessary
to separate myth from reality. Rather than a unitary concept, the
articulated public interest in large urban areas is evidence of a dialogue between different group and individual values and different
interests. More often than not, it is also indicative of the dominant
strength of some publics (some values). The vote is only one tool in
achieving a definition of public interest, and often only to ratify that
interest.

Here again, the value systems and the interests of representatives
of the poor, of the black community, have not found easy introductions
to, and a sustained role in, the dialogue.

5. Even if priorities and programs were matched to the needs
and priorities of the poor, the question of minimal involvement would
lessen impact. Alienation from city hall and from the dominant community stems not only from ineffective delivery systems and products,
but from an absence of involvement in planning, programing, and controlling that system and product. It may be unfair to picture the
present relationship of most cities to most ghetto areas as white
colonialism. Yet, if the resident of the ghetto assumes that this is
reality and acts accordingly, facts do not matter. That this assumption
of colonialism is common is testified to by every interview schedule
completed by our firm in every area of the country. It is also supported by the findings of the National Advisory Commission on Civil
Disorders.

> First, there is a widening gulf in communications between
> local government and the residents of the erupting ghettos
> of the city. As a result, ghetto residents develop a pro-
> found sense of isolation and alienation from the processes
> and programs of government.
>   . . . Ghetto residents increasingly believe that they
> are excluded from the decision-making process which
> affects their lives and community.
>   The political system, traditionally an important
> vehicle for minorities to participate effectively in de-
> cisions affecting the distribution of public resources,
> has not worked for the Negro as it has for other groups.[5]

6. The key to effective citizen involvement in ghetto areas is
the ability of local groups and individuals to convert local aspirations
into highly visible, creditable projects; in other words, to influence
the course of the public and private resource stream. Without this
constant conversion, citizen involvement quickly degenerates into
personal conflict and subsequently terminates altogether. "Why
come out to meetings—or go downtown—if nothing happens? . . . I
got no time. . . . What's the use?"

7. Aggregation and analysis of facts involve application of one
or more value systems. One set of facts can suggest to different
decision-makers alternative conclusions and policies. Further, decisions as to whether to amend or exclude facts are apparent in different options relative to defining public policy and programs. Time,
resource, intellectual, and value constraints prevent public or private
planners from presenting the range of possible alternatives that
emanate from a given set of facts.

THE DEFINITION AND ROLE
OF ADVOCACY

Earlier, a plea was made that planners, particularly city planners, redefine "planning" in terms of a resource-allocation process
which takes place within the physical environment but does not necessarily concern itself primarily with that environment. This plea was
combined with a comment concerning the irrelevancy of over-all,
long-range, coordinated planning and the relevancy of what was called
functional and micro planning. Irrespective of the selected planning
process, urban decision-making processes were described as adaptive, as incremental, and as evincing the contention of many groups
and interests. In this milieu, facts and values were not easily sepa-
rable.

If this frame of reference (which appears to be in accord with
reality) is linked to a value system which defines poverty and discrimination (class and caste) as the number one priority of urban
America, then the assumption of the advocate role is a claim on the
professional. The claim is strengthened if the professional perceives
cities as reflecting political economies of scarcity.

Advocacy in this context has a generic and even a modest meaning. That is, the planner, whether public or private, has a responsibility to present alternatives in such a way that the impact on the poor
and the ghetto resident of decisions pertaining to resource allocation
will be clearly recognized. Further, he would have at least the
minimal responsibility of submitting program alternatives (if they
are within his particular frame of reference) which indicate a benefit/
cost relationship in favor of the poor and the ghetto resident. In
essence, traditional concern for general city amenities, community
aesthetics, vehicular access, health, should be complemented if not
subsumed by concern for the priorities (physical, social, and economic)
of the poor and the translation of these priorities into effective programs.

More than this might well be asked of many professionals, particularly those who are committed to using their technical expertise
to convert the probability of an American tragedy into the possibility
of an American dream. If the premises outlined are accepted, then
there is ample justification and support for planners to serve ghetto
groups in a professional relationship. The objectives of such a relationship, which follow specifically from the premises, are:

1. To facilitate a redirection of existing and a direction of new
public and private resources to meet the priorities and needs of the
client group

2. To facilitate the matching of available resources to realizable client objectives

3. To facilitate introduction of the many and varied value systems of the client into the local decision-making process

4. To facilitate inclusion of ghetto groups and individuals into the local decision-making process

5. To facilitate the full exposition and discussion of alternatives pertaining to resource-allocation decisions and their impact on client objectives, priorities, and needs.

Advocacy could very well be called "technical assistance." It implies evolutionary rather than revolutionary changes in the institutional or delivery system. It suggests neither contention nor coalition as a permanent relationship between the client group and other groups (public and private). Indeed, these terms should be viewed as suggestive of strategy only and not as ends in themselves. Alternatives with respect to client response would vary by issue, by community, by stage in the planning process, by available resources and recorded priorities, by various group and individual involvement and alignment.

That advocacy can take many forms and shapes, once the professional has made the "great leap forward" of linking value to fact, is illustrated by some of the experiences of my own firm, Marshall Kaplan, Gans, and Kahn. To date we have been involved in several advocacy situations, in many of which we followed patterns usually considered in academic journals as pure advocacy; that is, in a direct professional-client relationship to a ghetto group. In addition to these assignments, however, we have also advocated what we thought to be the interests of the poor as best we could determine them in direct-client relationships with communities. This might be called "nondirected" advocacy or "advocacy by commitment." Between the purist role and the nondirected role, we have served in hybrid capacities. In many instances, that is, our contractual relationship was with a city, but the city asked us to work with a local ghetto group to translate their objectives and priorities into live programs.

In only one situation, that at Hunter's Point, was there contention, and this was viewed by the client, a ghetto group, and by us as strategic and only for the moment. Contention was easy to achieve, less easy to terminate. With the client's acquiescence[6] we released a technical housing report proposing the immediate initiation of a community-owned housing development on ten acres of vacant land in the urban renewal project area. To do this would have required a redefinition of Title I boundaries to exclude the land in question. Apparently, the redevelopment agency saw this proposal as completely alien to its plans. The director of the agency voiced his violent personal reaction even prior to reading the report.

Regardless of the merits of his later position, the intensity of the man's premature attack set the stage for an open public dialogue and helped strengthen community support for the client group. At this point, then, the clients had achieved two of their objectives; the first being entrance[7] into the resource-allocation game with respect to what they called their environment; and the second, the creation of more visible community support.

Some of the arguments raised following the release of the report have bearing on the issues discussed here. In criticizing the proposal, the agency's consultant, an outstanding local architect, raised the "problem of building housing units at the entrance of the Hunter's Point site." We countered by suggesting that this was a proper use, given the agency's commitment to making this primarily a residential community that would offer existing residents new housing choices consistent with their needs and priorities. It is worth noting that the now published agency plan provides for similar residential use. The agency stressed that to carve ten acres from the land included in the redevelopment plan would hurt the over-all planning program and would destroy the rationality of the anticipated project plan. This argument revolves around the sanctity of the general plan, its inviolability to change and amendment, as well as the priority granted to physical as opposed to social and economic objectives. In practice, renewal boundaries are changed every day during the planning process. That the Hunter's Point planning process had not even begun, suggests that the agency had great flexibility in defining or redefining project boundaries. Other issues were raised by the agency in contending with our client's plan. Those that dealt with comparative economics were quite pertinent. On the whole, however, none made the client's plan inappropriate.

They chose contention as a way of energizing their own organization and to assure that their value system, and their interpretation of facts, entered the public dialogue. This was done successfully. While contending with one public body, the redevelopment agency, they were trying to cement alliances with other public bodies and private groups as well as attempting to strengthen their own base in the community. Victory was not absolute for a compromise was involved; a compromise which was forced because neither the agency nor the client was certain of its strength; a compromise which was achieved by means of selective trade-offs acceptable to both disputants.

Contention, as we have said, is easier to engender than to turn off. The compromise resulted from many bargaining sessions involving city, redevelopment agency staff, federal officials, our firm, and representatives of the client group. When advocated before the client's board as the best possible political and technical resolution, the compromise, naturally, was not unanimously received. Some

wanted to continue the fight, thinking that more could be won; others
wanted to continue the fight, with the thought that even if all were
lost, the organization would be strengthened. Our role in the community was threatened because of our strongly held position in favor
of accepting the compromise. We indicated that this was the "best
the client could get under the circumstances (political and technical)"
and that "we believed success in achieving the compromise and in
later developing the units would do more to strengthen the organization
than continuing the conflict."

Life was not easy during those few days. Our ability to work
with the client was for a time jeopardized. Given the alienation,
suspicion, and hostility between the client and the agency, the feeling
of some was understandable. Given what we felt to be our knowledge
of the redevelopment process, we could take no other position. Final
judgment as to the correctness of our stand must remain open.
Similarly, what we would have done had the client chosen to disregard
our advice can only be subjected to unnecessary speculation. The
internal issue was resolved and the compromise finally ratified by a
majority.

In most other instances where we have assumed an advocacy
position, whether pure or nondirected, our clients, public and/or
private, have striven to strengthen an existing coalition between
themselves and/or other community, private, and public groups, or
to achieve such a coalition. Indeed, our role was seen as that of
facilitating creation of this coalition in that, as technicians, we could
supposedly help translate objectives and priorities relative to the
physical, social, and economic environment into realistic programs
which would combine public and private goals. Dialogue, albeit
abrasive at times, substituted for overt contention. Through successful
resource allocation, as in the instance of Bedford-Stuyvesant, involved
citizen groups solidified their base in the community, a base which
would permit them later to choose, should that be necessary, a different strategy than coalition on individual issues or, at different
times, in the planning process.

"Nondirected advocacy" perhaps best describes our work on
the Oakland model cities application. It is fair to say that in Oakland,
as in most other large cities, the poor, particularly Negroes, feel
alienated from, if not completely outside, the decision-making process relative to the allocation of resources. Indeed, the physical
ecology of the city—hills occupied by white affluents, separated by
limited access freeways from flatlands occupied by blacks—is, in
most residents' views, white and black, remarkably similar to the
social and political ecology.

Our selection by the city to assist a city-county task force to
prepare what was to be a successful application stemmed from our

working with the redevelopment agency on a scheme to restructure
the physical environment with minimal displacement and maximum
resident equity options. In implementing this assignment with the
agency, our values concerning the need to minimize relocation were
premised on interviews with residents and several factual analyses
of the impact of prior urban renewal plans in Oakland and other cities.
These values were related to, and supported by, the then new redevelopment agency director. The final report submitted to the Director and
his agency won some local and national attention. It was purposely
written to conform to what our office thought would be the format of
the application for the as yet nonexistent model cities program.[8]
To prepare the application, the city manager created a joint
city-county task force and asked us to serve as staff consultants.
The strains, cross currents, tensions, and resolution of tensions
engendered in the process of preparing the application were indicative
of the institutional and political milieu in Oakland.

The model city guidelines stressed meaningful citizen participation during the pre-application period. Yet, HUD allowed the cities
only four months from publication of its criteria to submission of
their proposals. While there was no doubt that Oakland might have
chosen other alternatives to gain citizen involvement, given the
juxtaposition of time pressures and difficulties in defining successful
participation models, the city made, we felt, a reasonable and honest
attempt. It chose to rely on interviews for priority definitions and
on the community action agency for dialogue with, and ultimate
ratification by, the residents.

The model cities legislation and criteria provided the normative
frame of reference for the pre-application work, a frame of reference
quite different from that of earlier federally financed planning efforts.
We saw our role as that of assisting the city in developing objectives,
priorities, and programs consistent with the program guidelines and
with what we thought to be priorities for residents of the area.
Discussion was lively and more than often tense. Our position as consultant to the task force was blurred, and we became thought of, and
thought of ourselves, as staff. We provided an evaluative reference
point for task force-initiated proposals, particularly those which
appeared on cursory examination to depart from the guidelines. In
the end, the city used us to create a dialogue with the residents.

It is fair to say, I think, that even if Oakland had not been a
successful applicant, the model cities pre-application process would
have been worth the effort. While no basic changes were made either
in institutions or in delivery systems in this short period, tentative
public commitments were made to rearrange some local priorities,
some local programs. All department heads participated for the
first time in a sustained process which focused their attention on the

needs of a particular area of a participating group of people.
While some proposals in the document may represent only a marginal
commitment by one or more local departments, these proposals, now
public, at least provided the residents with fresh opportunities for
dialogue and granted citizens who participated in the planning process
a frame of reference and, if needed, a bargaining position.

Oakland's present difficulties in successfully inaugurating the
planning process substantiate one of the prime criticisms which could
be leveled at nondirected advocacy. That is, given the felt alienation
of most residents in Oakland's model cities area it was probably a
mistake for us to provide a daily substitute for face-to-face involvement with residents in the planning process, however imperfect that
might have been. While it is probable that priorities for residents
implicit in the document are accurate, their involvement in deriving
these priorities was by choice and necessity minimal and confined
primarily to ratification procedures. How this could have been increased, given time and budget constraints, is open to speculation.
Hindsight provides easier answers than were apparent at the time.

We have attempted, with broad brush strokes, to present a critique of the city planning process and product and, in so doing, to
outline the premises that support advocacy and to define the role of
the advocate. In essence, the role of the advocate was defined partly
by the premises themselves and partly by the experiences of the
author.

1. Citizen participation: myth or reality. If participation is
defined by numbers, efforts to engender participation of ghetto residents in local decision-making processes have achieved only a
peripheral success. In most groups there is the symbol rather than
the reality of participation, and they have created a number of more
or less militant black leaders. This is perhaps no mean accomplish-
ment. Ghetto organizations have many of the characteristics of
nonghetto organizations, including fluctuating and crises-oriented
membership roles, shifting and varied constituencies, and lack of
sustained responsiveness.

To these similarities are added some differences, varying in
intensity, which emanate from the social, physical, and economic
environments. For example, members of many ghetto organizations
are experienced in or favor only limited strategies when playing
the resource-allocation game. Alienation, suspicion, and hostility,
compounded by lack of experience, reduce the political strategies
and limit the use of bargaining, negotiation, and compromise. Class
rather than caste issues produce serious internal conflict in some
groups, such as renters and owners, while the continuing conflict of
matriarch versus patriarch for control and dominance creates
instability. Like more affluent communities, the black community is

in reality many communities. As in more affluent groups, the quest
for personal leadership and personal recognition is apparent.

No easy answers exist for the professional as he works with his
client. He must continuously resolve, as with any client, the question
of his and the client's integrity. Because of the open-endedness of many
assignments, he is subject to the charge of being too aggressive or,
conversely, of being slow to respond, too "rational" in attempts to
define and develop strategies and programs. He must constantly be
aware of his own as well as the client's fallibility.

2. The white professional. The question of whether the white
professional can work with black clients, given existing racial tensions,
is difficult to answer. That we have been able to do so with some
limited success stems from our willingness to let the client group set
the frame of reference. This includes the normative definition of our
role as well as the process and product to be engendered. We have
usually required written contracts and included a provision that we
could be released on twenty-four hours' notice. This is done primarily
to create the image and substance of a legal and not a paternal relationship, and to establish trust between us and the client. While the
dismissal clause is probably unique, it is, we think, sensitive to the
need of the client to feel secure with respect to our motives.

3. Commitment vs. ideology. The reintegration of fact with
values is a necessary precondition for planners who jump into advocacy.
The value system assumed by the planner need only be a basic
humanism, a humanism concerned with expanding the choices of the
poor as a priority imperative. Values or commitment should not be
confused with ideology. Too often those with ideologies, whether of
the Right or the Left, use the poor rather than are used by the poor.
Given the complex problems facing the poor, plans premised on
ideologies are at best irrelevant and at worst harmful to the specific
interests of the poor, for they represent unreal, often misplaced,
abstractions. As such, they provide a shaky foundation upon which to
engage in the resource-allocation process. Finally, the planning
process engaged in by the ideologue must be, because of the nature
of ideology, a deductive one, whereas complex ghetto problems require an inductive approach.

DETERMINING LOCAL PRIORITIES

We commented that we now think we erred in assuming that we
could convey the objectives of residents of West Oakland to the city
task force and into the application. To err is human. In this case,
we based our actions on an internalized value system. Model city
guidelines in regard to timing gave us relatively few alternatives.

In essence, the issue was not so much the correctness or incorrectness of our estimate of needs, but the need, given Oakland's history, for direct community involvement. Even if we had "hit the nail on the head" and had been able to bring about a perfect coincidence of citizen needs and proposed plans, the lack of sustained participation would have caused conflict.

The perplexing problem, however, is that the conclusions drawn from rethinking Oakland's experiences do not fit all cities. In some communities where similar sequences of events occurred, forced again by exogenous factors like federal deadlines, the opposite results accrued. In these instances, our reading of objectives and priorities apparently conformed to that of most of the residents. [9] This fact engendered a coalition rather than an abrasive relationship with city hall. At this time, the only conclusion we can draw, and it may be premature, is that the historical response of city government to ghetto needs and the style of the present city government affect the response of residents to nondirected advocacy.

Whether advocacy is directed or nondirected, the professional should not think that it is easy to determine local objectives, priorities, and needs. Marginal dollar concepts fail, since all dollars are marginal. Ordinal and/or cardinal rating systems are difficult to achieve, given again prescriptive scarcity, and psychic strains resulting from decades of discrimination, that inhibits ready communication.

We have had some success in developing interview[10] schedules which appear to gain insight. In addition, we have striven for direct working relationships with a range of ghetto organizations including our client groups. In the end, however, rationality is not complete, and we must rely on reasoned intuition and the veto power of our clients.

Modest claims are made for advocacy, defined as technical assistance to public and private groups premised on a commitment to a particular class and/or caste in society—the urban poor. This commitment is a necessary precondition to assumption of the role. Yet, the commitment should not be viewed by the planner as heroic; for it is now assumed to be, short of our debilitating exercise in Vietnam, one of the nation's top priorities, certainly one recognized in the model cities legislation. Advocacy defined as such should be viewed by public officials and ghetto groups alike as a positive factor, for it could help convert destructive behavior into constructive dialogue.

NOTES

1. "At-large elections" refer to the election of city councilmen by the entire city electorate rather than by specific neighborhoods or subcommittees.

2. Whether we like that reality or not.

3. Charles E. Lindblom, "The Science of Muddling Through," Public Administration Review, XIX, 2 (1959), p. 80.

4. Report of the National Advisory Commission on Civil Disorders (New York: New York Times Co.; Bantam Books, 1968), p. 2.

5. Ibid., pp. 284, 286, 287.

6. No formal vote was ever taken. The organization at that time was having internal problems. Once our report was completed, a majority of Board members agreed to its release prior to submittal to city hall. We concurred. As indicated, the rationale for release was: (1) to open up the public dialogue; and (2) to use the dialogue to strengthen the community organization.

7. Entrance did not guarantee that they would win the game, but it did grant them a position.

8. Congress enacted the model cities program shortly after the publication of the firm's report to the redevelopment agency.

9. Or at least those who expressed a view.

10. We have experimented with both black and white interviewers and have no clear-cut preference with respect to results.

CHAPTER

6

COMMENTS
ON THE
DEMONSTRATION
CITIES PROGRAM

Implicit in the Demonstration Cities proposal is the recognition that the nation's efforts at urban renewal leave much to be desired. Indeed, although cost-benefit analyses have portrayed eventual fiscal rewards for some communities, and while skylines of others may have been embellished by architectural monuments, the often attendant social and psychological effects on those displaced cast the wisdom and political efficacy of the program in doubt. Attacked by both the right and the left, renewal had no strong center. Whether or not the Demonstration Cities program will serve cities better than the renewal program is open to conjecture. Two elements in the Demonstration Cities legislation, one implicit and one explicit, lend cause for initial optimism: First, the method of determining the amount of the ultimate grant to be given and, second, the apparent intent of the Federal Government to "deliver the inventory."

1. Determining federal allotments: Although by a somewhat circuitous route, the Demonstration Cities legislation makes it possible to provide cities with what is in effect a block grant.[1] Carried to its fullest, the approach may grant cities necessary flexibility in meeting growing physical, economic, and social problems.

2. "Deliver the Inventory": Coupled with the commitment to provide cities with a massive infusion of new aid is the commitment to make available the existing inventory of federal programs. Obviously, this inventory is extensive. No real effort has been made, however, to piggyback existing programs in innovative combination or to saturate selected disadvantaged areas with a carefully planned

---

This chapter originally appeared in Journal of the American Institute of Planners, November 1966, pp. 369-71.

and programmed infusion of available federal resources. Because of
the disparate use of existing programs, there is no leverage to
maximize program benefits—or, as in the case of urban renewal, minimize the program's social costs. Selection of different packages of
federal programs and different strategies for their use in order to
achieve preselected social, economic, and physical objectives, while
possible, has been difficult, given the institutional pluralism in Washington and in local areas.

To expedite the coordinated use of federal programs, the
Demonstration Cities act provides for the creation, in each locality
having an approved comprehensive city demonstration program, of an
Office of the Federal Coordinator responsible to the Secretary of the
Department of Housing and Urban Development. It is the intent of the
authors of this legislation, rather than its actual provisions, that
provides the rationale by which HUD can deliver the inventory on time
and in the proper sequence. Indeed, the legislative language immediately following the section authorizing the coordinator defines his
real authority only in terms of delegated functions that emanate from
HUD. The coordinator's prime role will be, in effect, to grease the
transmission belt; to bring the client and the appropriate department
or agency together; to persuade rather than to mandate. Whether or
not this will be sufficient is a moot question. To achieve what the bill
intends, coordinated use of federal programs, real direction and real
leverage will probably have to come from the Secretary of HUD and,
ultimately, from the White House.

The departures from the existing pattern of federal-city relationships called for in the funding of the program and the coordination
of existing programs are worthy of the label "Demonstration." While
there is sufficient wording in the Bill to indicate that HUD will not be
receptive to communities which submit merely an aggregation of
renewal projects, the Bill's orientation to central city problems in not
immediately clear. Given the effect of the debilitating war in South
Vietnam, as well as other national needs, it is probable that the gen-
erous federal aid promised cities in the opening paragraphs of the
legislation will not measure up to expectations. Local decision-making
will therefore continue to function in a political economy of scarcity.
Priorities will need to be set, given a diminishing local resource base.
Decisions will still have to be made, despite whatever federal largess
is available, about what areas and what people in the city will benefit
from any new allocation of outside resources. A good case could be
made that despite noble intentions, urban renewal benefited those that
have more than those that have not. If this is not to happen with respect
to Demonstration Cities, then HUD's direction will have to be strong
and clear.

Because of the location of the program in HUD, housing and

community development will probably be its prime target. Yet readings of the priorities established by residents of disadvantaged areas indicate that the physical environment, including housing, while important, are less so than jobs, income, and education. If housing, is nevertheless, to be a key element in the Demonstration Cities program, then the emphasis ought to be on devising techniques—technology and funding—to permit the poor to remain in their present locale if they desire to. This suggests a much greater emphasis on rehabilitation than heretofore. It also indicates the need for much greater discretion in the use of existing federal programs, particularly Title 1. For example, if Title 1 could be used together with Sections 115[2] and 312,[3] successful rehabilitation for lower income families may be possible. In many respects, the problem is analogous to a normal clearance project. The writedown, however, would not be premised on the expected re-use of cleared land, but a rehabilitated structure for low income residents. In effect, the writedown would be sufficient to permit the cost of shelter after rehabilitation to be within reasonable rent or cost-to-income ratios of projected owners or tenants.

President Johnson asked in his message that the "demonstration be managed in each demonstration city by a single authority with adequate powers to carry and coordinate all phases of the program." When translated into the Bill, this admonition becomes less stern. Cities need only have "administrative machinery" available for carrying out the program on a consolidated and coordinated basis. Despite the mild reduction in concern for managerial finesse, the warning is clear. Cities, to be selected as a Demonstration, must be structured to implement the program within a six year period.

It is to be hoped that HUD's concern with proper management and efficient administrative machinery will be complemented by concern that localities create entities that are politically responsive and accessible to the electorate, particularly that segment of the electorate residing in the demonstration area. Second, initial soundings from Washington suggest that a city may be required to prove its capability to successfully administer the program even prior to the first year planning grant—a discouraging situation that might negate whatever value the initial year study grant (and the promise of more) could have in moving cities that presently do not have a "proper" framework for effectuating the program. Certainly, forcing cities to create an administrative structure at the outset of the first year will have the effect of limiting the ability of local residents to participate effectively in the program. Indeed, unless one believes (somewhat unrealistically in light of the social structure of most disadvantaged areas) that the principle of countervailance will work to create a viable resident response to city actions concerning the demonstration program, time will be needed to develop an effective relationship between local citizens and the entity created to implement the program. This relationship should not be precluded by fixing the structure too early in the game.

Both the President's speech accompanying the Bill and the Demonstration Cities legislation make a strong commitment toward inclusion of local residents in planning, development, and implementation, but this commitment will be difficult to fulfill in a meaningful way. Both the workable program requirement of Title 1 (the Urban Renewal Program) and the recent efforts of the CAP programs to broaden the base of the War on Poverty indicate the friction costs associated with problems of citizen participation and local control. Of various issues involved, three come immediately to mind: whether local residents will have the power to veto a program; whether they will be included in the planning process in the early planning stages; and whether they will have a piece of the action when plans begin to be translated into reality. These issues become all the more difficult to resolve when one tries to define the leadership of the poor or to enumerate so-called indigenous groups. They become insurmountable in cities in which local government is not structured to be politically responsive to minority residents.

Historically, most planning practitioners are physical determinists in an area in which physical determinism has no simple meanings, and positivists in an era in which positivism is irrelevant. Planners have for years practiced in an aseptic environment. Plans have reflected aggregate numbers rather than the more important needs, objectives, and priorities of individual neighborhoods, groups, and communities. Where planners have taken part in the general debate over the allocation of resources in a city, the effect has more often than not further disadvantaged those already denied choices open to most others. Acceptance by the planners of a somewhat organismic concept of the city, one in which only middle class values are recognized, has impeded a real understanding of the city. Concentration on the general plan, in theory and practice, has directed them toward consensus in an environment in which consensus over most vital issues is impossible and toward a level of rationality and abstraction quite irrelevant to urban life.

The Demonstration Cities program suggests a planning process quite different from that practiced by most planners. Instead of planing for residents of the city, planners will have to plan with them. Instead of viewing the city in a generic fashion, they have to establish for specific areas housing specific people. Since most of the households in defined demonstration city "areas" will be, in Melvin

Webber's* terms, "place people," the planner will be forced to substitute a concern for the microenviroment for the more traditonal
concern for the macroenvironment—an environment in which social
problems will have to receive a higher priority than physical problems.
To be effective, the planner will have to understand and have a facility
for working with a wide variety of federal programs. Finally, he will
have to concentrate on the here and now, not the distant future. Unless
the planner is capable of playing by the new ground rules—unless
he is willing to relate to urban issues—the Demonstration Cities
program may not be, in effect, his ballgame.

NOTES

1. This might be interpreted as a modest variation of the so-
called Heller plan which sought to provide such grants from the federal
government to the states. Purists might suggest that the Demonstration Cities program limits grants to the confines of an approved plan.
Yet, if planning requirements are as comprehensive as indicated in
the federal criteria, the supposed limitations on municipal expenditures
will be minor.
2. Section 115 (Grant Provisions): Rehabilitation grants can be
utilized individually or in combination with other programs. These
grants of up to $1500 are available to low-income individuals or fam-
ilies who own and occupy a one- or two-family residential structure
located in a Title I urban renewal project or in a concentrated code
enforcement area.
3. Section 312: Owners of property within a Title I urban renewal
area or a concentrated code enforcement area (Section 117), may be
able to receive loans of up to $10,000 for a period not to exceed 20
years. The interest rate is 3 percent. To become a recipient, applicants must show an ability to repay the loan and must indicate an
inability to secure financing at such comparable terms.

---

*Professor of City Planning, University of California.

CHAPTER

7

THE ROLES
OF THE PLANNER
AND DEVELOPER
IN THE NEW COMMUNITY

For some years, the popular press has been deluged by professional and lay articles critical of the way people were choosing to
structure the physical environment. Opprobriums such as slurb,
sprawl, and scatteration have long been utilized by planners to describe
the effects of the urbanization process. It has become rather the conventional wisdom to look at America's landscape and cry "alas, it
could have been different. If only we had rational planning techniques."
Generally, the culprits range from those "evil speculators," those
under-capitalized but over stimulated builders, those boys at city hall,
those unincorporated areas, those fourlegged personalities—the automobiles, and finally, those people.

By 1960 the cry of protest had grown loud. Indeed the planner
had picked up powerful allies: the downtown interests, the cityphiles
and the intellectuals. Yet "for all the chorus of protests, most
Americans seemed strongly unaroused. Each year they buy a few
hundred thousand picture windows, seed a few hundred thousand lawns."[1]
Indeed, "for millions of suburbanites, their post-World War II experience has been prosperous and open far beyond their depression-born
expectations. For them, the suburbs have been one vast supermarket,
abundantly and conveniently stocked with approved, yet often variegated,
choices."[2]

Just when the battle against the twin dangers of sprawl and
scatteration appeared hopeless, the planner found new allies (apparently

This chapter originally appeared in the Washington University
Law Quarterly (St. Louis, Mo., Washington University Press, 1965)
pp. 88-104.

stronger than all others) in the New Community and the new community
developer.

THE NEW COMMUNITY

With a seeming burst of enthusiasm, House and Home Magazine
informed its readers that "across the United States there are at least
75 completely planned communities of 1,000 or more acres where
developers are creating facilities to house more than 6 million people.
. . . All this is hard to grasp since most of these new towns differ
radically from the kinds of communities that most housing community
people have created in the past."[3]
Newsweek rather idyllically asked its readers to picture a town
where children walking to school need never cross a street, where
homes and apartment houses overlook a park or lake, where unsightly
telephone wires and television antennas lie deep under ground. A
Utopian model at a world's fair pavilion? the magazine asked. And
it answered: not at all. At least twenty[4] such communities offering
most of these features are now being built from Virginia to California.[5]
Still another writer has said:

> the new community as we are beginning to visualize it,
> offers a solution to many of the most pressing problems
> in our environment in happy interacting combination. In
> answer to urban sprawl and the shortage of land—not in the
> country at large but in easily accessible desirable places—
> it offers concentration. . . . It thus gives people the sense
> of identity, of sharing that is lucky in the anonymous vast-
> ness of our cities and suburbs.[6]

To facilitate the private initiation of these three-dimensional
panaceas, thus impeding "sprawling, space-consuming, unplanned and
uneconomic" development, the federal government recommended in
1964 a program whereby the Federal Housing Administration would
insure loans made to developers for land acquisition and development
needs. Apparently Congress did not reflect the "winds of change"
blowing in the nation, for the proposals relative to New Communities
died in committee. Expectations are that the same bill will be submitted again and this time meet a happier fate. The privately-developed
New Community is to become a weapon in the battle to achieve the
Great Society.

THE PRIVATE DEVELOPER—EVERY
PLAYER HAS A NUMBER

General Description

Differences exist among New Community developers which affect
organizational structure, operational processes, funding of development
needs, perceptions of future role in the development of other communities and method of land acquisition. Yet there is at least one characteristic generic to all the developers. Although some would attach
more emphasis to it than others, they would all agree that making money
is one of their prime motives. Whether this urge is expressed in terms
of a cash flow position or an ultimate profit yield (or both) depends on
the corporate or personal state of the developer concerning such complex items as the holding costs of the land, market perceptions, and
over-all tax situations.

Most developers seek to confine their activities to acquiring the
land, planning the community and then pre-servicing the land with
water, sewer, and other public facilities. They are not true community
builders, and they hope, in effect, to market furnished lots to builders.
Expectations are that the primary source of profit[7] will emanate from
land appreciation accruing to the development because of its planned
community image and the availability of community services. Additionally, they see the builder as willing to pay a premium to be buffered
from local political pressures.

Whether done on intuition or by analytical process, almost every
developer to some extent has made a reading of the nation's increasing
affluence, and of the increase in disposable income and leisure time
available to most consumers. These socio-economic factors are
reflected in the amount of amenity usually included as part of the
New Community package. "Color it green" is a virtual admonition
of all developers to their planners. To the reflections of the developers,
the planners have added their concerns about imageability, defined
geographical edges, balances and housing mix. When the concerns of
the planner are felt to be reflected positively in the market place, the
developer articulates the best the planner has to offer—often in more
understandable language.

Types of Developers

Most New Community developers fall into two major classifications. The expansionists see themselves as able (and willing) to initiate

several New Communities (and other real estate developments) at one
time and are indeed contemplating continuous replication of New
Community projects. Conversely, the non-expansionists do not appear
to be looking beyond their current activities.[8]

Expansionists

Sunset International Petroleum Company[9] and Janss Corporation[10]
perhaps most readily characterize the expansionist class. These com-
panies perceive themselves as having developed sufficient expertise
to operate in a wide number of development areas. Indeed, both have
developed skill in funding land acquisition and development needs.
Although consultants are called in from time to time, necessary
market and planning studies are most often prepared in shop by their
own personnel. Both are experimenting with the computer as an aid
to decision making.

Non-Expansionists

The non-expansionists have gained most of the favorable national
publicity relative to the development of new communities across the
country. Like their compatriots the expansionists, they operate on
either newly acquired land or land owned or controlled by them for
some time. Their style of operating is generally much more personal
than that of the expansionists and decisions more often than not are
made on a more intuitive and subjective basis. Highly paid and well
known economic and planning consultants are used more frequently,
thus reducing the need for staff.
   Among the non-expansionists, some have entered into the New
Community arena with the zeal of a missionary, determined to bring
to Americans a better way of life—a way of life they seem willing to
define with some certitude. These developers appear much more
willing than others to experiment with both design and social infrastructure. Two of the leading missionaries are Robert Simon, developer
of Reston, just south of Washington, D. C., and Jim Rouse, developer
of Columbia, just south of Baltimore, Maryland. Simon sees the
community as providing people with an area where they "should be
able to do the things they enjoy, near where they live." He adds that
"Reston will provide many Americans . . . the stability of belonging
to one community for a lifetime. They are tired of rootlessness."[11]
According to one commentator, residents of Reston will have little
need to move from the city. "Simon's town will provide a home for
every phase of the cycle, without once moving out of the magic circle
of Reston. It will eliminate the need for forming four or five sets of
friends during a lifetime and offer, along the way, the marvelous

mixture of wisdom and nonsense, of grave responsibility and youthful hijinks present in every small community."[12] Rouse is far less a physical determinist than Simon. Thus Rouse has been far less pedantic and self-conscious about his planning or his debt to urban design and architecture. Instead he has concentrated more on the very tenuous relationship between physical and social planning. His community, by providing people with a better environment (better defined in terms of both social services and physical amenity) and improved communication linkages (accessibility of ideas, people, and goods) will be a "garden for people, God-centered" and an environment hopefully replete with love.

Other than the missionaries, two other breeds of non-expansionist developers exist—the entrepreneurs[13] and the land lovers.[14] Like the missionaries, both articulate the fact that their New Community will lead to the "new way of life."

Although the missionaries have come to believe their own speeches, the entrepreneurs treat the new community primarily as a marketable product. Indeed, their commitment to a "new way of life" parallels quite closely their view of what will sell and is not generally the result of any prior normative commitment to an overview of society. Conversely, the land lovers see the new community primarily as a means of preserving the values imputed to be inherent in the land itself—values often connected with a lengthy period of prior ownership and threatened by the rush of urbanization.

THE DEVELOPERS' VIEW OF PLANNING

The degree to which most New Community developers have manifested a narcissus complex in their relationship to planning is striking. The almost unanimous willingness on the part of private entrepreneurs to identify with the "benefits" of a planned community emanates in part from their perceptions of the market, of human behavior, and of political structure. Additionally, the developers, through the process of osmosis, accepted the "environmental truths" handed down by professional planners and others relative to the need for open space, balance, mix, order, etc. This acceptance was premised on perceived psychic and material benefits in marketing the planners' paradigm.

The Plan as a Philosophy

The beginning of a plan for a New Community must be a philosophy and not topography—not existing zoning and

other ordinances of the community, not public financial
regulations or other factors dealing with the money
market.[15]

To a greater extent than the other types of developers discussed
earlier, the missionaries and the land lovers treat their project as an
extension of their own personalities and philosophy of life. Simon,
nurtured on the values of English New Towns, exposed to the philosophy
of individuals like Mumford and Stein, views a community's physical
environment as playing a very important role in the formation of
human as well as group personalities. Reston is an expression of
Simon's philosophy relative to the importance of the community as a
physical envelope. Rouse also is quite articulate when expressing his
personal philosophy relative to the meaning of community.

> Personally, I hold some . . . conclusions to the effect that
> people grow best in small communities where the institu-
> tions which are the dominant forces in their lives are
> within the scale of their comprehension and within reach
> of their sense of responsibility and capacity to manage.[16]

Because Rouse and Simon, despite corporate trimmings, are the
moving force in their respective projects, their objectives will provide
a ready framework for the planners—especially those planners historically fed by the logical positivist.

Similarly, developers of the Irvine Ranch have a predetermined
philosophy relative to the inputs into the planning process. Unlike
Rouse and Simon, the content of the input reflects not a physical
determinism or a self-conscious attempt to relate social and physical
planning, but a "feeling" for the land. The result in its effect on the
planning process, however, is the same. In essence, the developer's
philosophy is fed into the planners' stream of consciousness.

The Plan as a Reaction Against
Environmental Criticism

Developers are not unaware of the continuous stream of criticism
leveled at the emerging physical pattern resulting from the urbanization
process. When the New Community was posited by the planners as
an alternative to "sprawl" and "slurb," the developer was at least
receptive. When the alternative was perceived to be a competitive
package—competitive in terms of creating dissatisfaction among
households in existing units and as a magnet drawing in-migrants
away from older or other new units—then the developers' initial

receptivity changed to enthusiasm. Profits and doing good became synonymous. The developer and the planner spoke the same language.

The Plan as a Reflection of the Market

While society at large may judge a developer a success or failure on the basis of a benefit-cost equation which includes physical as well as socioeconomic criteria, success to the developer is measured primarily in terms of his ability both to maximize and optimize income. Given present institutional and market factors, a developer's fate is measured more by return on equity and cash flow than by the degree of social inputs or physical amenity included in the plan. That many developers are inclined to link potential profits with the marketability of a new way of life must be attributed to their reading, whether right or wrong, of America's affluence and changing pattern of living.

Basically, the New Community developer has received the same stimuli which caused larger builders in the late 1950's to reorient their production from moderately priced to higher priced housing. In addition to the almost unanimous feeling that the market for lower priced houses was and is thin, most developers have acted on the assumption (sometimes conscious, other times sub-conscious) that early sales to lower income households impede efforts to sell units to higher income households. Moreover, a heavy initial increment of lower priced houses is thought to hinder establishment of a proper fiscal base necessary to support development of community wide services. Whether these perceptions are true is not relevant. What is important is the fact that community developers base their decisions on the assumption that they are true. Thus, few new communities currently being planned and programmed will include housing priced at less than $20,000. Furthermore, most community plans reflect in their land use allocations and internal design a concentration on the felt needs of the more affluent members of society.

To the developer, the plan offers an additional and useful means to assure (and insure) consumers that their investment will be protected and that they will be able in time to "trade up" on equity—a very important factor attendant on the purchase of a home in a New Community. The plan reduces environmental uncertainty or, more aptly, offers environmental protection. Thus it serves as an effective Miltown pill to anxious buyers worried about the future of their investment. In effect, they will be able to play the Great American game called "house appreciation" or "moving up in the ranks."

For much the same psychic reasons the plan plays a crucial role in attracting investors. To the investor, like the consumer, the plan represents a developer's reflection of the market and his proposed

strategy to capture that market. Although the investor may (or may
not) be more sanguine than the consumer in measuring the developer's
ability to implement the plan, the plan at least offers the investor a
product and a measuring rod.

The Plan as a Political Instrument

Most developers feel that preparation of a long range plan is
imperative in localities where the political powers are either unfriendly
or where the political winds of change blow frequently. The plan once
agreed upon by both contestants—developer and politician—provides
the developer with a definitive road map. In the developer's view,
the plan protects the project from meddling political gamesmen.

Where public officials are more receptive to the projected New
Community, the plan serves a different political function. Here the
developer and the local officials jointly use the plan as a means of
boosting the attributes of the area. Both hope the new development
will be a container of industry and homebuyers (particularly those
homebuyers who are rich). In those cases, growthmanship suits the
needs of developer and politician alike.

Preparation of a plan may become crucial if the developer
contemplates using any federal programs in a privately developed
New Community, for attached to almost all federal programs is a
comprehensive planning requirement. Although most non-urbanized
counties do not meet federal planning requirements, it is quite possible
that the developer's plan may prove a ready substitute once it is approved by the public agency.

TYPE OF PLAN AND PLANNING PROCESS

Despite each developer's announced intention to produce a different environmental package from what already exists, and to produce
the only real New Community in America, there is a surprising same-
ness about the general physical plans which have been prepared by
most New Community planners. Most communities are generally
divided into three elements: neighborhoods, villages, and town centers
(the exact nomenclature attached to the various community subdivisions
may change from community to community, but the principles are the
same). Villages are oriented around a central area supposedly programmed to meet the needs of residents for impulse and durable goods,
as well as to supply any need for vicarious urban pleasures. There
is a hierarchy of physical components, each representing a different
order of social activities.

Each order of physical unit from neighborhood to town center will have commercial, educational, and recreational facilities commensurate with the proposed population and its ultimate needs. Surrounding each village will be open space; surrounding each community will hopefully be some kind of a buffer either in the form of a greenbelt, or an arterial system. Balance, self-sufficiency, and housing mix are all part of the lexicon found in New Community plans. Housing mix usually refers to a variety of housing types and to some variation in the price range. Balance and self-sufficiency are often defined in terms of land set aside for the hopeful arrival of (clean) industry and for the development of recreational as well as various commercial facilities. People will then be able to live, work, and play in the community.

Each community is rather self-conscious about the amount of recreational facilities and "open space" included within its confines. Parks, trees, golf courses, swimming pools, bridle paths and "restful play space" are all important means toward achieving the new way of life and the sale of houses.

A developer's personality, his philosophy (or lack of one) relative to the ideal community, his view of the market and his perception of the local political scene will determine the extent to which he will "buy" the services of the planner and his over-all approach to planning. When these elements are in internal conflict or do not accurately mirror external realities, the final plan may not only reflect schizoid tendencies but limit the viable alternatives open to the developer. Additionally, when the developer's perceptions of the market are inaccurate, an inability to react quickly may be fatal. Yet a lengthy reaction time may be forced on the developer because of the political necessity to have a defined plan. Those who view the market as a buyer's market and see the plan as a merchandising tool will probably prepare quite definitive long range plans.[17] Also, the need to "lock in" the community to protect it from political interference will lead a developer to prepare a precise plan.

To date, most New Community plans have been of the precise type; in these cases the planning is neat, rational, logical, and fixed. The range of alternatives open is quite limited. Implicit in this approach is the treatment of the New Community as an end product, with an initial development year and a terminal point. That the community will change, will develop, will redevelop after "1980" is acknowledged by the planners, but often denied by the plan. Every area is planned, with little flexibility provided in the design for unforeseen events. Obsolescence—either planned or unplanned—is not a considered input.

In juxtaposition to the type of planning described above is the nonplanned community. Here the developer apparently is more

concerned with being able to react quickly to changes in the market
than with the need for potential protection from less than understanding
politicians. No matter what the market conditions, he prefers flexibility in future actions over a plan which might limit alternatives because
of public or resident acceptance. To this type of developer, the plan
represents a salt shaker, and land uses, the contents. These uses
may be shifted around or "shaken up" almost at will depending on the
initial reaction of the market.[18] In most of these communities, land
values replace land use as the primary input into the planning process.
Precise general plans for the entire community are scrupulously
avoided, replaced by plans showing only enough detail to carry the
developer through the initial development years.

RELEVANCE OF THE NEW COMMUNITY

    Is the New Community a way toward a brighter tomorrow,
deserved of replication across the land scape? Or is it merely a
historical anachronism, pleasant and nice, but socially, economically,
and physically irrelevant? By present standards of community planning,
most of the privately initiated projects win high applause, and if implemented, they will be aesthetically pleasing both to the resident and
to the visitor. Yet the platitudes currently being received by the
private developer must be tempered by knowledge that the communities
presently being planned will house primarily upper income, white
Americans.[19] These citizens are perhaps least concerned with the
"self-contained," "balanced," geographically biased concepts implicit
(if not explicit) in all the New Communities.
    Increased affluence and technological advances have widened
the work, play and living choices of the majority of Americans. Spatial
boundaries no longer serve as effective barriers limiting communication or circumscribing the range of one's interests. While the appella-
tion "Jet Set" may still only fit a limited few, the term is quite symbolic of the growing irrelevance of space or place in defining community. Perhaps a new definition of community is needed, one that con-
centrates on non-spatial, non-place elements.[20] In effect, the
frequency, duration, and intensity of communication linkages between
and among people would replace the more traditional metes and
bounds definition. Each individual, able because of income or intellect
to play the non-place game, would have a hierarchy of communities
at his disposal.
    This paradigm does not reflect the way of life for the "have nots"
in society, but for the majority it is quite an accurate picture. It is
just this majority which will be the supposed beneficiaries of the new
way of life created within and by the New Community. Primarily

because of their locational freedom and diversity of linkages, they
will have a low order of shared interests within their new place of
residence. Most will be members of other more viable communities,
not geographically located within the confines of Utopia, U.S.A.

The import of the local community will differ, of course, depending on the individual household and the members of that household.
No doubt women with small children are locationally bound, but even
here the extent of community linkages is usually defined in terms of
morning coffee and a baby-sitting pool. Nobody is inclined to take
in another's washing—at least not for too long.[21]

Neither the developer nor the planner is content with the
increasing choices open to consumers of housing space. The spatial
emancipation of human beings is frowned upon, and terms like balance
and self-sufficiency are posited as an ideal. The developer is more
pragmatic than the planner. While the planner holds on to his English
New Town legacy, most developers interpret "balance" as meaning
any amount of industry which can be cajoled into the area, and self-
sufficiency as meaning fiscal insulation and a proper tax base. Even
those New Community plans which define balance as "a number of
jobs equal to the resident labor forces" do not project every resident
as working in the New Community. Thus, a flow pattern will continue
to exist between and among communities. The journey to work will
not be abolished and the freeways will still be useful.

What of the place people—those whose choices are restricted
because of low income, color, or subculture and who will not be found
in great numbers in the New Community? Given the place orientation
of these citizens, even marginal efforts to improve their physical
environment might have a much more meaningful effect than such
activities will have on the more affluent. For the affluent, the
residence-community nexus is but one among many; for the poor, it
is the primary one. Additionally, for the affluent the way of life
purchaseable in the New Community cannot be too significantly different
from what they had before.

Perhaps the most common and more cogent defense of New Communities lies in positing such developments as an alternative to urban
sprawl, scatteration, and slurb. Here the rationale rests on some
"best urban form," although to argue the best physical form for a
metropolitan area involves us in a never-ending debate over benefits
and costs. The debate often degenerates into subjective evaluation
and meaningless shibboleths. "Neither scatter nor compaction are
wholly a hero or villain, but each may have its place in a different
scheme of values."[22] Although sprawl may result in greater public
costs for public facilities, it does provide a needed flexibility in meeting
future development and redevelopment needs. Space is left internal
to metropolitan complexes and each area is developed over a

differentiated time period. As contrasted with the New Community, sprawl provides lower income families an opportunity to play the game of choice relative to the environment.

In many respects, the land use ingredients in these New Communities will not be too different from the ingredients found in "non-planned" communities built during the last decade. During the 1950's, for example, dispersal of industry into privately- or publicly-sponsored industrial parks gave suburbia a job base. Locational freedom provided by freeways made the journey to work palatable, linking places of residence and place of work together quite compatibly. New markets brought shopping centers and services to the suburb. Thus, through the independent decisions of many builders, industrial developers, shopping center developers, local governments, and the consumer, new suburban "communities" come into being. Although planners and academicians may not judge the result as meritorious, it worked.

Certainly the New Community offers a better micro-environment, a better mix of environmental ingredients and a locational arrangement for that mix which reduces accessibility costs to residents. However, the real test of these New Communities is whether they facilitate or impede choices. The community must not only serve as a resting place for those individuals seeking to escape from the freedom available in the market place, but more significantly the community must serve as a take-off point, a launching pad permitting residents to enter the non-place hierarchy of communities.

THE NEW COMMUNITY AND THE PLANNER

Given the social, economic, and physical ambiguities inherent in the New Communities, it is surprising to witness the almost unanimous unquestioned approval granted these developments by planners and the rapid migration of planners from public to private employment. This tendency is odd in a profession that has been described as "reasonably weary of cultural definitions that are systematically trotted out to rationalize the inadequacies of city life today, for the well-to-do as well as for the poor."[23]

> To many planners, fortunately, the challenge of the city
> is meat and drink, but others, appalled at the chronic
> disorder of it, have turned their eyes outward and
> dreamed of starting afresh with new regional towns.
> These, the hope goes, would be more severed from the
> city than today's suburbia; clean and manageable, each
> would have an optimum balance of activities, would be
> nourished by its own industry and have an amateur

culture of symphony orchestras, art schools and little
theatres, all its own.[24]

That the city planner should look with "green" eyes at the
current crop of New Communities is on close reflection quite understandable. More than other professions, the planner has been pre-
conditioned by two long-standing beliefs: the first in physical determinism,[25] the second in the relevance of the general plan. Both are
out of tune with the complexities of city life, but both lend themselves
quite well to the New Community.

Physical Determinism

Historically, the planning profession has been dominated by the
designers, architects, and engineers. From the Chicago World's Fair
of 1893, our history by choice is one of non-involvement in the politics
of a city. Our philosophy is steeped in an errant logical positivism,
our marching orders have been city beautiful, city practical, city
economic, and only recently city social. Planners have seen the city
through the eyes of a nominalist as a collection of neat functions,
prescribed by rigid physical dimensions. They have concentrated too
long on urban forms as an abstraction rather than on the relation of
urban form to the lives not of a homogenaic population but of a hetero-
genaic population which includes the Negro, the single person, the
aged, the divorced, and the widowed.

Many planners still hold fast to the doctrine that there is a
definite and provable correlation between the physical environment
and social pathologies. That there is not an easily defined relationship
between the physical environment and human behavior is now quite
apparent.

> The simple one to one cause and effect links that once tied
> houses and neighborhoods to behavior are coming to be
> seen as but strands in highly complex webs that, in turn,
> are shaped by the intricate and subtle relations that mark
> social, physical, economic, and political systems and
> their associated behavior. The simple clarity of the city
> planning profession's role in this is thus being dimmed
> through clouds of complexities, diversity. . . .[26]

The General Plan

The planner oftentimes solves all the big problems while ignoring
the small ones. As a result, the planner's relationship with the city

often ends in alienation. The city looks for a stronger, more helpful ally, while the planner continues his search for a more fertile hunting ground—where he can practice global decision-making.

Although this analysis may sound too fatalistic, it does reflect the growing ineffectiveness of city planners in large urban areas. Existing cities will play a vital role in serving "the rest of society at present and for the immediate future as a combination Ellis Island and training school for the receipt, training and ultimate transshipment to the suburbs of underprivileged inmigrants."[27] Implicit in a view of the city as a place where acculturation takes place is a commitment to view the city not as an abstraction, but as people, different people who must for the time being play out their lives (or their game) inside its narrow confines.

Given the planner's latent heritage of physical determinism and his philosophical acquiescence in logical positivism, he is uniquely at a disadvantage in playing the city game. In a dynamic, mobile urban society, where politics is at best incremental and serves as a safety valve for the strivings of different groups, the long range general plan positing a comprehensive goal system and emphasizing physical form in terms of defined edges and neat internal areas serves only as a salutary device at budget time. Conceptually, the long range planning approach is impossible for it cannot be "practiced except for relatively simple problems and even then only in somewhat modified form. It assumes intellectual capacities and sources of information that men simply do not possess and it is even more absurd as an approach to policy when the time and money that can be allocated to a policy problem is limited, as is always the case."[28] Moreover, in order to reach a consensus (the main thrust of the long range plan as a political tool), goals must be reduced to a community-wide and jointly shared value base. Those sharing, however, are the most articulate and powerful, often not the growing minority of city residents (the poor, the Negro). The acceptance by the planner of a somewhat organismic concept of a community, one in which really only middle class values are acceptable, negates his very effectiveness in the process of decision-making. To the disadvantaged, the immediate present and not the distant future is most relevant. Conflict is essential if they are to participate in the distribution of society's benefits. The long range plan often mutes the complexities of city life, impedes a realistic view of a city's problems (its peoples' problems) and provides little in the way of help for decision-makers.

Unable to understand the functions of cities or of the people within them, planners have always responded favorably to the Garden City and New Town idea. Not only are these alternatives physically oriented, but they are premised on the belief that a good environment will produce good people. Additionally, since there are often no people

on the site and the landscape is left untouched, the general plan
approach may work. The planner is again useful and his view of life
brightens.

SOME ALTERNATIVE ROLES FOR THE FUTURE

The almost universal applause granted New Communities by
the planner is an outgrowth of the historical evolution of the profession
and its subscription to the general plan approach. That New Communities will result in a prettier landscape is accepted almost as a
truism; that they are in tune with economic and social trends in this
nation is open to debate. It behooves the planner to participate in that
debate if his profession is to remain a vital one. Whatever the outcome,
however, the planner needs to redefine this role if he is to make a
contribution towards improving the lot of his fellow men. Perhaps
the physical environment in macro-scale may not play as significant
a part in promoting human welfare as was once thought. Beauty and
amenity are values, but they are quite subjective values. Urbanization
will continue, and should be accelerated in order to facilitate the distribution of benefits to lower income households. Debate over urban
form and urban structure should be relegated to the classroom (and
competing computers). "We should not engage in pep talk slogans
like save the city or clean up the slums. I care very little about the
city as a physical element and I don't hate the slums, per se. I want
to know what is wrong with our economy, our education, our health
services, our counseling, our housing programs, our transportation,
and what we can do about it to expand opportunity in both the city and
the suburbs."[29]
In the non-place world, the affluent treat the old concept of
community quite carelessly. People and establishments are constantly
breaking through the paper confines placed on them by planners and
sociologists. Conversely, because of the general plan concept and
approach, those people who are place-oriented receive the fewest
benefits from planning, and are often harmed because of the planners'
broad brush strokes.
If this analysis is correct, it suggests that planners should re-
focus their attention away from the whole, the general, the corporate
and the communal aspects of the city. Emphasis should be on planning
as a resource-allocation process and criteria should be prepared to
assist in the dispersion of public goods and the direction of private
growth. Equal treatment in terms of time or expenditures will not be
available to all areas of the urban complex. Problem areas must be
identified by the planner, and a choice of alternatives must be presented
to the community.

The prime objective of the planner will be "to seek to induce those patterns that will maximize the accessibility of the cities' residents to the broad range of opportunities for interaction that advanced civilization opens to them."[30] Three special areas will demand this attention: (1) the reduction of the friction cost—the communication costs—for the non-place citizen, (2) the improvement of the physical environment for place people—the disadvantaged, and (3) the planning of micro-spaces as a psychic commodity.

In terms of reducing friction costs, the planner will concern himself primarily with facilitating the movement of people, goods, and ideas. With respect to the place people (the poor), planners will concern themselves with the type and level of marginal physical improvements necessary to enhance the viability of their areas as take off points, and as reflectors of positive personal and community images. Finally, intimate space is important to both the place and non-place people. For the place people, proper environmental space may mean the difference between total alienation and personal and community integration. For the non-place people, space represents a "resting place" from participation in the hierarchy of communities outside the residence community. It also represents a place where he can escape from the freedom of his everyday world from time to time. Planners know little about the effect of micro-space and structure on either the human or group personality. Yet in terms of the way man plays out his game, the small world may be more important than the larger one.

Departure from the general plan concept and acceptance of the approach to planning defined in this article suggest a much closer relationship between physical and social planning. While there is not a one-to-one ratio relative to the effect the physical environment has on social behavior, complex cause and effect relationships do exist.

Social planning can make a significant contribution to the welfare of urban residents by the careful analyses of the impact of physical changes on human beings. If planning for the physical environment is thought of as instrumental to the achievement of social ends, then the artificial barriers created by nomenclature such as "social" and "physical" will be broken.

It is foolish to argue that physical planners have a role which frees them from concern as professionals with difficulties facing society, such as poverty, social disorganization and the like. Despite an aggregate affluence, decisions made within our political and institutional framework are guided by an economics premised on scarcity. Every physical input into the environment represents an allocation of resources. Goods and services dispersed in one area, may not be spent in other areas. Additionally, while planners may have only a limited chance to "do good," they do, through ill-conceived recommendations, have an opportunity to do tremendous harm to the ecology of people and environment. How New Communities are implemented by planners and developers will thus have a critical impact on the allocation of environmental resources in improving the welfare of our urban communities.

NOTES

1. Raymond Vernon, The Myths and Reality of Our Urban Problem (Cambridge, Mass.: Joint Center for Urban Studies, 1962).

2. David Riesman, Metropolis: Values in Conflict 71 (1964).

3. "New Towns for America," House and Home, February 1964, p. 123.

4. Newsweek was quite modest in its enumeration. Over one hundred so-called "New Communities" are presently in the planning or development stage in the United States. Generally, in terms of the developer's goals, a New Community can be defined as a planned development on many thousand acres, incorporating a hoped-for complement of residential units, industry, and commercial establishments.

5. "New Communities," Newsweek, Nov. 23, 1964, p. 112.

6. Wolf Von Eckardt, "Could This Be Our New Town?," New Republic, November 7, 1964, p. 21.

7. Almost all of the developers express an intention to hold on to certain investment properties. For example, most will lease or rent commercial space and multi-family units.

8. Perhaps another way to classify the developers relates to their method of land acquisition. There are two distinct classifications: developers who are operating on land which they have owned for a long period of time and developers operating on recently-purchased land. Each of these categories symbolizes different funding needs, different development strategies and different cash flow problems. Both categories may be utilized to describe further the expansionists and non-expansionists today.

9. Sunset's major operation in the New Community area is in Sacramento-Sunset City. The company purchased an option to the 12,000 acre site in 1960 and exercised this option in 1961.

10. Janss's major new community endeavor is at Conejo, forty miles northwest of Los Angeles. The land (8,000 acres) has been controlled by the Janss Company for many years.

11. "The Reston, Virginia Story," Washington World, August 17, 1964, p. 8.

12. Ibid., at 27.

13. A good example of the entrepreneur would be Allan Lindsey, developer of El Dorado Hills, north of Sacramento, California.

14. A proposed New Community is being developed on the Irvine
Ranch near Los Angeles by the Irvine Company. This property has
been owned by the Irvine family for a great many years. In essence,
the land has become an extension of their personality.
15. Address by Robert Simon, Developer of Reston, Virginia,
to the Anglo-American Seminar on the Planning of Urban Regions,
Oxfordshire, England, July 1964.
16. Interview with Jim Rouse, April 1964.
17. As indicated earlier, the land lovers and the missionaries
see the community as an extension of their own personalities and
their own philosophies. They have a tendency to view the community
more as an identifiable product—one that is easily translated into
two-dimensional form. Thus they would be quite likely, completely
apart from market or political factors, to seek translation of concepts
into definitive plans.
18. This type of planning may make it more difficult to sell a
community to potential homebuyers. Uncertainty is increased if the
homebuyer cannot see his neighbors as well as the relation of his
neighborhood to other neighborhoods and other land uses on the plan.
19. This is stated primarily as a fact and not as criticism.
Most developers are correct in their readings of the market. The
judgment that the market for lower priced housing is thin in fringe
areas seems correct. This is primarily due to the lack of jobs in
the suburbs, and the availability of adequate housing in older areas.
Given our present institutional framework, the developer cannot be
held responsible for cases of extreme poverty.
20. Melvin Webber, "Explorations into Urban Structure," in
The Urban Place and the Nonplace Urban Realm 79 (1964).
21. The elementary school has no doubt provided a focus for
strong "community" linkages. But even here changes in the educational
system related to social pressures (civil rights) and educational innovation (team teaching, educational complexes) may make location of
the elementary schools less subject to specific geographical criteria.
22. Jack Lessinger, "The Case for Scatteration," Journal of the
American Institute of Planners, XXVIII, 3 (August 1962), p. 159.
23. David Riesman, The Lonely Crowd (New York: Doubleday,
1953).
24. William Whyte, The Exploding Metropolis (Garden City,
N.Y.: Anchor Books, 1958).
25. The planner is in the rather unique position of first denying
and then affirming a role. As a physical determinist, he is in this
game to improve peoples' lives through improvements in the physical
environment. When asked which people, he will submit, perhaps
reflecting the influence of the logical positivist, that this is not his
problem to decide. Some planners would argue that planning is "good

in and of itself," and has little affected resource allocation or the
distribution of benefits and costs.

26. Melvin Webber, "Looking Toward an American Institute of
Planning Consensus on Professional Goals 2," Draft Paper for American
Institute of Planners, Washington, D.C., May 16, 1963.

27. Bebout & Bredemeier, "American Cities as Social Systems,"
Journal of the American Institute of Planners, May 1963, p. 68.

28. Charles E. Lindblom, "The Science of Muddling Through,"
Public Administration Review, XIX, 2 (1959), pp. 79, 80.

29. See comments by Edward Eichler in "Segregation, Subsidies,
and Megalopolis," An Occasional Paper on the City, No. 1, 1964, p. 19.

30. Webber, op. cit. supra note 26, at 3.

8

**RANDOM THOUGHTS
ON PLANNING,
PROBLEMS,
AND APPROACHES:
SMALL CITIES**

It is unfortunately fair to state that, except in the Model Cities program, the principal beneficiaries of planning efforts have been the planning consultants. Certainly, the products of the planning have had only a marginal impact on the capacity of local government to improve the quality of local life.

Why is this so? Perhaps it is because of the marginal state of the planning art; perhaps it is because of the environment in which planning functions. Certainly, one of the reasons is that very few city governments have any real role or authority in the realm of planning. The aftermath of the Depression left small cities with little but house-keeping functions. That is, during the Depression Washington assumed responsibility for most social welfare functions—that had been until then either handled locally by the political party through the turkey basket at Thanksgiving or not at all. As the list of federal programs grew, states and counties rather than small cities became Uncle Sam's surrogates.

Devoid of responsibility in respect to social and human problems and limited by a lack of resources and the overwhelming impact of national fiscal and monetary policies in the economic area, small communities, generally settled back to do only physical planning. While providing many professionals with jobs and more consultants with contracts, planning efforts, geared neither to human problems and priorities nor to market factors, have rarely had more than a

---

This chapter originally appeared in The City, Its Resources, Structures and Systems, Proceedings of the 47th Annual Congress of Cities, December 7-11, 1970, Atlanta, Ga., pp. 53-56.

cosmetic effect. Yet there are now more than 45 separately funded federal planning assistance programs involving nearly $250 million.

Most communities have become involved in federally aided planning efforts for the purpose of securing related federal grants. That is, their commitment to planning is often only as strong as their desire for this or that grant that carries a planning prerequisite. As indicated earlier, this participation in federally funded planning efforts has not necessarily helped cities. Indeed, some instances, the city's ability to allocate scarce resources effectively has actually been reduced. Oakland, California, for example, has been for many years the recipient of numerous separately funded planning programs, but the city remained unable until recently to present an enumeration of problems, priorities, and programs. As implied, Oakland's city fathers, although not entirely without fault, should not be blamed altogether for this situation. For example, in Oakland, as in other cities:

1. Individual federal planning grants directed at Oakland were provided respective city, county, and state agencies without any review and/or sign-off by the mayor or the manager. In effect, it was almost impossible for the mayor and/or manager to develop a city hall planning capacity.

2. Programs often took no cognizance of the respective roles to be played by the mayor, the various agencies involved, or the residents. Indeed, federal guidelines were more concerned with the precise content of the plan than with the effect of that plan on local commitments, on local budgeting processes.

3. Grants were made without recognition of other "competitive" or related federally funded efforts, and programs carried on without knowledge of the impact of these efforts on one another and on the capacity of the city of Oakland to absorb such new money.

In effect, the "hodgepodge" of federal planning aids reflects more the growth of federal categorical programs and parallel local recipient groups than any recognized need to help cities build capacity at the local level. Only the Model Cities program provides, in effect, a direct grant to city hall for planning purposes.

New planning ground rules are necessary if local governments are to develop a local planning capacity for the allocation at scarce local resources. Some are proposed below that should allow small city mayors to develop, for the first time, a capacity at city hall to manage and strategically direct public and private resources to improve the quality of life in their communities.

1. Most mayors have spent too much time thinking about local planning structure instead of thinking about the roles of those who are to participate in and relate to that planning structure. Though a proper planning structure is important, _more_ important are the roles, assigned

the mayors, the planners, and the residents. If a mayor reneges on his responsibilities in the sphere of planning, he loses any chance to develop a politically realistic planning base; he loses any chance to develop an effective coalition with resident groups around planning issues and priorities; and he permits the professional planner to set priorities and define programs—which is really the responsibility of the elected office holder.

2. The planning game should not be given over to consultants. (HUD's 701 program has built many firms but not developed much in the way of city hall capacity.) Planning funds, whether local or federal, should be used to add competent staff, under the control or direction of the mayor. Consultants, if used at all, should come in only under the mayor's agenda, and for specific purposes.

3. Mayors should insist on reviewing and commenting on all federal planning assistance programs prior to their use in the city. Several key federal agencies now give the mayor this right, and others will soon do so. Even if they do not, local political (and institutional) clout provides you the price of entrance into the review game.

4. Mayors should insist on one planning process, and this process should have a clear link to the city's capital improvement and capital budgeting programs. One process need not always imply one planner. The mayor's prime concern should be that all the various planners in his city are at least communicating with one another; that issues are raised and debated; and that he takes part in their resolution. In effect, a good information system may be more important than a good plan or the brightest planners.

5. Mayors should mandate resident involvement in problem and priority selection as well as program development, recognizing that such involvement means participation by individuals who because of income or color have been traditionally denied such a right. Ground rules will be difficult to define. Yet, The Model Cities program has taught us that coalitions between city hall and residents—despite occasional tensions and unnecessary rhetoric (on both sides)—lead to a more realistic approach to defining needs and more appropriate and relevant priorities. As important, such coalitions engender positive changes in agency behavior.

6. Mayors and their staffs should learn how to function as grantsmen, a skill necessary for effective planning. They must come to know the federal and state participants and their programs. Even if state revenue sharing and consolidated grants are upon us (which is doubtful) city executive must still deal with their peers in Washington and the region and must still negotiate with their counterparts at the state level. Ours is a uniquely complicated system. Fortunately, or unfortunately, it will remain so.

7. Finally, Mayors should ask their planners to drop their pretenses, their jargon; they should simply fire planners who ask them to engage in "long range synoptic . . . linked . . . planning." Given the state of art, it is unrealistic, except in defining general policy objectives, to spend more than a marginal amount of time looking beyond a few years at a time. Further, the very size of the small city, combined with related resource limitations and institutional constraints suggests that planners should limit their attention principally to strategic areas of opportunity—areas on which the city can have an impact, whether economic, social, or environmental area. Efforts at comprehensiveness should generally be eschewed—or at least defined inductively. For example, should mayors, fortunately or unfortunately, be faced with the entrance of an industry into their nice clean towns, they shouldn't first rush to prepare a master plan that will be soon forgotten. What is needed is a hard and selective look at what the industry will mean in terms of different resident in-migration patterns, wage levels, class and caste problems, welfare and traffic burdens, taxes, and so forth. And these matters are not hard questions to fathom; the pluses and minuses become apparent without lengthy and expensive studies. As important as the plan of action that results from the examination of these factors is the process set up for studying them and the level of involvement in that process of those required to act on the findings.

The ground rules just mentioned clearly suggest a definition of planning vastly different from the one used in towns and cities. They suggest that home grown planners or consultants should not be relied on to produce a proper plan, a plan concerned primarily with the physical environment; they suggest that planning should be perceived as the strategic management of limited resources. Those who will participate in the planning process must include city hall, agencies, and residents. Staff should be used by the mayor primarily to help clarify narrow options and weigh discrete alternatives. As implied, planning should be directly tied to the budgeting process. Planning areas of concern should be identified on the basis of specific and narrow objectives, selected problems, and limited priorities. Institutional and staff capacity, as well as budgeting constraints, will weigh heavily in enumerating alternative work programs.

Development of local ground rules, should be complemented by new federal approaches that can assist in the development of local resource management capacity.

1. It is to be hoped that the federal government, given its reasonably positive experience with the Model Cities program and its disasterous experience with other federal planning aids, will move to consolidate all federal planning programs into a few open-ended capacity building plans and management grants. Appropriately, such grants would be

available only to elect state, county, or local officials. They could be
used by such officials to hire staff. And financial penalties in the
form of reduced grants should be provided if consultants are relied
upon to produce plans.

2. It is to be hoped also that a movement toward consolidated
block grants would not in all instances force small cities to deal only
with states, whose commitment and ability vary considerably. Options
should be open permitting small cities to become recipients of federal
funds without having first to apply to the state government. Direct
federal-city relationships and city-metropolitan area relationships
should be explored along with ways of improving city-state relationships.

3. It is to be hoped that the state revenue sharing proposal, if
finally passed by Congress, will provide small cities with funds based
more on need and population than on tax performance. Indeed, it is
worth while to consider converting the revenue share to a discretionary
block grant.

4. Finally, the federal government should develop a national
recruiting pool from which small towns could select professional
employees. Recruitment, training, placement, and initial wage supplements could be provided by the federal government.

9

MODEL CITIES AND
NATIONAL URBAN POLICY:
THE RELEVANCE OF MODEL CITIES
TO GENERAL AND SPECIAL
REVENUE SHARING

If the Administration proposals relative to special revenue sharing meet with Congressional approval, most of the categorical programs now being administered by HUD, as well as model cities, will be discontinued. A single, consolidated community development grant, to be provided to cities on an annual formula basis, would take their place. According to initial press accounts, city use of grant monies would not be limited, apart from Title VI, by extensive national performance criteria or complex federal administrative regulations.

In anticipating some of the major issues with respect to general and special revenue sharing, it may be helpful to relate these issues, where appropriate, to what we have learned about model cities.

MODEL CITIES: PROMISE
AND PERFORMANCE

Model cities became law in the fall of 1966. The program, according to the prevalent rhetoric, was to achieve in a five-year period nothing less than a dramatic social, physical, and environmental reformation of select blighted and deteriorating urban neighborhoods.

Essentially, participating cities were promised two types of federal assistance if they: (1) developed a planning and program coordination structure, one administratively responsible to the chief executive but with appropriate links to representative resident groups;

This chapter originally appeared in ASOP Proceedings (Chicago, American Society of Planning Officials, 1971), pp. 28-35.

(2) initiated a predefined rational, sequential, and orderly set of planning processes; (3) completed and submitted plans (products) reflecting "a concerted local attack" on a broad range of social, economic, and environmental problems in a city-defined model neighborhood; and (4) illustrated through their structure, processes, and products a set of federal performance standards (often undefined) relative to coordination, innovation, institutional change, and citizen participation. The federal assistance included model cities grants (called supplemental funds) and a share of existing categorical programs. The supplemental funds supposedly could be used to meet the costs of any innovative projects in the model cities plan and/or to help redirect or mobilize existing resources necessary to support identified model cities projects. Money from the categorical programs could be used to meet the basic costs of locally defined model cities programs.

Federal Role

On the whole, however, it is fair to say that the federal response to model cities has been inept. It has revealed the tremendous complexities inherent in the present federal delivery system. For example:

1. Congressional authorizations and appropriations for model cities have never matched the public hope of those who initially supported the legislation. For example, the $2,300,000,000 projected as necessary to fund 75 cities in 1966 falls far short of $2,500,000,000 authorized through fiscal year 1972 for close to 150 participating cities. Cumulative appropriations, assuming Administration current requests are met, will probably total less than $2,000,000,000 through fiscal year 1972.

Authorizations and appropriations do not tell the whole story. The hold of the Office of Management and Budget on the rate of obligations and expenditures (resulting in part form the Administration's anti-inflationary effort), combined with the cities' unanticipated problems in completing their plans and initiating programs, have impeded the rate of actual local outlays. At the present time, such outlays approximate less than one-third the level of available appropriations.

2. Neither President Johnson nor President Nixon lent the full prestige of the office of the President to the program. As a result, HUD model cities efforts to secure earmarked funds from federal agencies rested more on the tenuous persuasiveness of the solicitor and the responsiveness of program managers than the potential clout of either administration. Only HEW and HUD itself managed to

allocate a visible amount of money to model cities from any existing program. Yet even the sums given by these two departments were miniscule in comparison to the size of their respective inventories.

3. The prescriptive nature of federal department-local client relationships, when combined with bureaucratic resistance to change and the lack of real White House commitment to the program, prevented federal simplification of administrative criteria (i.e., "flexible interpretation of categorical programs") to meet model city program needs. For the same reasons, federal tolerance for local innovation and institutional change, as expressed in agency review of categorical program use and agency-provided technical assistance, was rare.

The above critique should not imply that no tangible and significant federal actions were initiated. HUD did resist White House and departmental pressure and reduce city choices concerning the use of supplemental funds. Similarly, efforts to make operational definitions of interdepartmental coordination should be judged heroic, given the existential quality of the federal world.

Such events, however, are visible primarily as anecdotes. They testify not to a national commitment but to the strength and resiliency of select individuals in key positions. They are important because they offer a way of roughly measuring how far interagency performance fell short of early promises. They support the need for alternate strategies at the federal level if a "concerted attack" is to be made on urban problems and if a program like model cities is to be given a chance to, in terms of legislatively mandated goals, improve the quality of life in our cities.

Local Role

Cities, on the whole, accumulated a far better model cities record than the federal government. Yet local model cities accomplishments, given the short history of the program and problems associated with the federal response, cannot and probably should not be evaluated or measured against "quality of life" objectives in the statute.[1] They should be viewed instead in terms of their local capacity building— their validity as instruments[2] in developing and improved local ability to meet locally defined objectives, needs, and priorities, particularly those of the poor.

Most cities had difficulty in meeting HUD's initial, overly rational planning and program implementation requirements. These requirements often appeared to local officials, staff, and/or residents to be inconsistent with one another. For example, in many communities attempts to achieve an operational definition of coordination seemed to limit or frustrate widespread citizen participation;

rational, orderly planning was thought in some cities to be antithetical
to innovative options; a general planning and management staff capacity
responsible to city hall seemed contrary to HUD process requirements,
thereby complicating the development of specific model city plan components; and normative criteria concerning institutional change seemed
impossible to achieve given the preference for project management
by existing institutions.

Despite problems, many of them related to local capacity factors
and others to an inept federal response, most communities succeeded
in completing at least their initial planning period and almost all have
begun to convert plans into projects. In the process more than a few
cities have: (1) developed, often for the first time, city hall-resident
coalitions sufficiently strong to identify problems and affect the distribution and use of public and private funds; and (2) developed, often
for the first time, a residual staff at city hall able to articulate a
locally relevant definition of coordination apropos to both planning
and resource allocation.

Each city's response to model cities appeared to fit one of five
categories or systems.[3] These systems were determined by the level
of turbulence in the environment, the role of the chief executive, and
the characteristics of the model cities resident group. For example,
with an involved chief executive and a reasonably strong resident
group whose members were experienced in public decision-making,
residents and staff were given an almost equal voice in the model
cities program (parity system). On the other hand, a weak resident
organization, when combined with an involved mayor or manager,
made city hall both the client and constituency of the staff and permitted
the staff to dominate the local model cities program (staff dominant
system).

If a high level of tension was evident in a city, the presence of
chief executive commitment alongside a cohesive resident group
provided the residents with the key role in decision-making. In these
instances, the local chief executive consciously chose to give way to
residents in order to avoid confrontation (resident dominant system).

Both residents and staff could do no more than influence the
model cities program in their respective cities if early in the program
there was little or no chief executive support and a weak resident
base. Who provided the primary model cities influence—residents or
staff—generally depended on whether chief executive involvement came
before or after the appearance of a reasonably strong resident group.
If the former came first, staff became the major influence; if the
latter came first, residents had the strongest voice.

Structural differences among cities did not appear to affect
basic response patterns. For example, the form of the city government and the organizational characteristics of the model cities agency

Systems and Their Determinants

Planning Systems	Degree of Turbulence	Chief Executive Involvement	Resident Characteristics
Staff Dominance	Low	Sustained	Internally weak Non-integrated[a]
Staff Influence	High	Minimal	Internally weak Non-integrated
Parity	Low	Sustained	Strong Integrated
Resident Influence	High	Minimal	Internally weak Non-integrated
Resident Dominance	High	Sustained	Strong Non-integrated

[a]Integration refers to the presence of members in the resident group with access to city hall; with previous experience in public decision-making.

(unlike the level of turbulence, the role of the chief executive, and the nature of the resident group) did not seem to determine the basic approaches to model cities. Significantly (particularly in terms of illustrating the relevance of model cities to issues related to general and special revenue sharing), each of the approaches or systems appeared to lead to different results. For example,

> . . . the staff dominant system was able to more closely conform to HUD's process requirements than the others. They were, unlike most cities, able to complete their plans within the one year planning period. Further, in doing so, they followed with some conscious variations, HUD's orderly planning process; and introduced the use of professionally oriented techniques. While all systems had trouble defining and responding to HUD's criteria concerning innovation, institutional response and resident involvement, parity and resident dominant systems illustrated more evidence of these performance criteria than others.
>
> Cities in the parity system evidently were able to translate better than others, Federal mandates pertaining

to coordination and resource mobilization/concentration.
They were, for example, able to involve a greater number
of agencies, for more than limited periods of time, in
efforts to develop common strategies concerning planning
processes and products. Subsequently, they were also able
to project greater reliance on categorical programs as a
proportion of their total budget.... [P]roducts submitted
by cities in parity and staff dominant systems appeared to
come closer in form if not always in content to HUD defined
criteria. Finally, the planning program in cities initiating
either a staff or resident influence system departed more
than all others from HUD's prescribed planning approach.[4]

It seems that the parity system offered the best odds for success
in meeting model cities objectives. It is also clear, if we identified
the correct system determinants, that the federal government could
have, if they had wanted to, played a more conscious role in helping
cities define local systems.

MODEL CITIES AND REVENUE SHARING

Like revenue sharing, model cities reflected, at the time of its
passage, a major departure from the categorical program system.
Cities were promised money free of most of the restrictions traditionally associated with federal aid efforts. Unlike revenue sharing,
however, particularly as articulated by the President and his sub-
ordinates, model cities required cities to initiate and/or complete
certain actions prior to funding.
    Because of the historical linkage between model cities and
revenue sharing it is important to relate model cities' experiences
to the issues now beginning to emerge concerning revenue sharing.[5]
These are: (1) the presence or absence of performance criteria; (2)
the amount of federal discretion in determining annual fund levels for
state and local government; (3) the national level of funding for both
programs; and (4) the nature of the recipient.

Presence or Absence of
Performance Criteria

The President, during his State of the Union message, indicated
that Title VI would be the principal, if not the only, performance
criteria governing federal monitoring of general and special revenue
sharing funds. Since that time, the Administration's thinking has

apparently evolved to the point where it is considering adding nominal planning requirements to at least some of the special revenue sharing programs. Some sort of maintenance of effort or comparability requirement for local allocation of education funds in poverty areas or for low-income households is apparently now acceptable.

Those who have argued for additional performance criteria concerning, for example, development of local capacity and the level of local expenditures for the poor have been told that definition of such criteria will ipso facto lead to a return to "onerous and detailed categorical program criteria." This response certainly distorts the intent of many of the proponents of performance criteria who, like myself, are severe critics of the way current categorical programs are routed to recipients. More important, it seems to blur the distinctions between performance and administrative criteria and in so doing ignores what we have learned about performance criteria from the model cities program.

The President should be applauded for his efforts to give state and local government more freedom in the use of federal funds. Such endorsement does not, however, necessarily include support for the development of programs which provide money completely free of any strings. State, county, and local governments often need more than a little prompting to tend to certain national interests, particularly those related to the poor. Many mayors would, in fact, welcome the shelter of such statutory prompting.

These performance criteria, as distinguished from administrative regulations, do not have to define detailed operational or content characteristics associated with the use of federal money. Based on our analysis of varied model city approaches and the seeming predictability of the results, they can be used to encourage achievement to objective concerning: (1) an areawide management/planning process linked to resource allocation;[6] (2) the nature, type, and extent of involvement of elected chief executives in local management/planning and resource allocation efforts; and (3) the nature, type, and extent of participation of residents, including the poor, in local management/planning and resource allocation efforts. I also would ask that recipients of special revenue sharing funds allocate a significant portion of their money to meeting national concerns, giving particular attention to the needs of the poor.

With the above performance criteria, general revenue sharing could provide the "bribe" necessary to permit local governments to mount an effective war on poverty for the first time. In effect, communities could trade off funds provided by general revenue sharing with poverty directed funds from special revenue sharing. If the balance of payments was not convincing to local constituencies, chief executives could always fall back on statutory language—a protective safeguard of some value to mayors participating in model cities.

The performance criteria proposed here would eliminate most
present federal reviews concerning what cities spend their money on.
They would, in effect, still permit achievement of Administration
objectives for overhauling the existing delivery system and, at the
same time, strengthen our ability to meet commonly accepted national
objectives.

Federal Discretion Versus
Formula Allocation

Justified criticism of often unpredictable grant allocation methods
and their impact on cities, combined with the laudable desire to provide
cities with more freedom in the use of federal urban assistance programs, has lead the Administration to opt for formula allocation for
general and special revenue sharing. A major share of the funds of
both programs would be allocated to communities on an annual basis
according to formula. Pre- and post-audits would in most instances
be limited to fraud and Title VI.

A regularized grant process would be a welcome one. This is
not to say, however, that the federal government should relinquish
primary discretion over the general level of specific grants to each
community. Such a proposition seems premised more on faith than
on city experience, more on political theory than political reality.
Alternate approaches consistent with the need for selective performance
criteria in revenue sharing could be taken by the Administration. Each
should be compatible with the principle that cities ought to know in
advance how much money they have to plan with and that cities meeting
select national objectives should be able to determine the end product
associated with grant money. For example, cities could be provided
with an earmarked sum of money (either by way of a "pass through"
or directly from the federal government) based on such single or
multiple indices as tax yield and the range of local social, economic,
and environmental problems.[7] Precise fund levels, however, would
be subject to clearly enumerated performance criteria. Federal reviews, unlike model cities, could be reduced in most instance to pro-
claimers of intent and post-audits relative to accomplishments.
Possible variations might include: (1) providing all recipients with
a base level of funding, free of performance criteria (supplemental
funding would be premised on acceptance and achievement of stated
criteria); (2) providing recipients with differential levels of funding
based on performance of specific criteria.

Any general distribution formula agreed upon by Congress
should allow for some federal discretion as to the total amount of
grant funds offered state and local governments. Recipients should

(and can) be left with considerable freedom as to the specific use of
federal funds.

National Level of Funding

Both the general and special revenue sharing packages appear
to reflect a new commitment by the Administration to meet the growth
and revitalization needs of this nation. Several real allocation problems, however, are on the horizon, suggesting the need for further
analysis and possible major increases in funding. For example,
although funds from general revenue sharing would provide the base
upon which state and local government could develop the capacity to
plan, manage, and supplement the more functional oriented special
revenue sharing monies, initial calculations suggest that only a few
cities will receive more from general revenue sharing than they
already receive from a single model cities grant. Similarly, funding
for the special revenue sharing program appears quite nominal given
the immensity of local needs and the fact that fund allocations will
not be constrained (as in model cities) by neighborhood boundaries or
aggregate population limits. Hold ("harmless") clauses, while
perhaps necessary given previous commitments and political realities,
suggest two somewhat juxtaposed or contrary dilemmas. First, they
may skew funding away from cities that need money the most; second,
they may, particularly given present budget ceilings, obviate the
ability of high capacity cities to secure funds based on performance.

Nature of the Recipient

According to the press, the Administration is still debating the
terminal point of general and special revenue sharing. Apparently,
some are opting for including other than elected chief executives
(e.g., districts, agencies, etc.) as possible grant recipients. No one
seems to have really answered the tough question of how to fund areawide entities and special districts, particularly if these groups do not
meet the approval of relevant general purpose local governments.
My own position is that only the offices of general purpose state
and local governments should be grant recipients. All other government agencies should then secure their money from the state and
local governments. Only in this way can we test the ability of general
purpose government to develop operational definitions of management
and coordination which permit an articulation of priorities and trade-
offs between competing agencies' objectives. Only in this way can
we produce the type of public sector resident coalitions (parity system)

which, based on the model cities experience, offers the best hope for
the distribution or redistribution of public monies paralleling the
needs of all residents.

NOTES

1. These objectives while laudable were in retrospect quite
unrealistic (even assuming model cities was the correct programmatic
tool) given the lack of national commitment.
2. This does deny the fact that many interesting and perhaps
ultimately significant projects have been initiated by and in model
cities. The importance of these projects, however, in meeting local
problems or in serving as national prototypes must, given the lack
of history, remain quite speculative.
3. System is defined as an observed pattern of related events,
actors, and issues. It should be understood that observed determinants
could change over time and therefore characteristics associated with
each system could change.
4. Marshall Kaplan, Gans, and Kahn, The Model Cities Program
(Washington, D.C.: U.S. Government Printing Office, 1970), p. 68.
5. The President in his message to Congress concerning special
revenue sharing for community development clearly identified model
cities at least as the precursor of this part of his proposed legislative
package.
6. Planning and management of resources, assuming that there
is a locally relevant definition of coordination, could become the focus
of a needed debate over short-term objectives, priorities, and allocations. In effect, the planning process, if linked to budgetary considerations, can become an appropriate field of battle, negotiation, compromise, and/or direction.
7. The administration's present formula for general revenue
sharing provides a near equal split between states and cities, with the
latter receiving an automatic "pass through." Tax yield is used along
with population to distribute funds. I would propose adding indices
related to poverty in order to avoid skewing distribution of funds to
wealthier communities. I would also set the upper level of fund allocations to states and communities on the basis of achievement of identifiable performance criteria.

10

PLANNING
FOR PEOPLE:
HUMAN RESOURCES,
PROBLEMS, NEEDS,
AND PROGRAM ALTERNATIVES

Since the AIP decided, somewhat reluctantly (and happily), about a decade ago that proper median strips and widths of curves and gutters did not necessarily constitute improvements in the quality of people's lives, there has been a spate of papers and speeches about the need for planners to think more "comprehensively"; to "integrate" physical planning with social planning; to relate more to people; and to plan along with people, not always for people. While many pens have been set in motion—including the author's—it must be admitted that planning remains more an art than a science; that concern for the specific needs of specific groups living in cities remains outside the content of most general plans.

Unfortunately, no ultimate solution will be presented here; merely the reflections of one who has had the opportunity to assume alternatively the role of evaluator of national, state, and local social planning efforts and the role of adversary in discussions concerning the same at local, state, and national levels.

A BRIEF HISTORY

Unlike many European countries, this nation has never accepted more than limited responsibility for the social well-being of its

---

This chapter originally appeared in the American Institute of Planners' Conference on Government Relations and Planning Policy, January 26-28, 1970 (unpublished).

residents. For example, initial efforts at social planning, emanating
as they did out of the Depression, were seen by most as only residual
elements in a game plan concerned primarily with surmounting national
difficulties. World War II, understandably, focused attention on issues
unrelated to domestic needs. Competition between Congress and the
Executive—complemented by apparent ideological divisions, often
more weighty in rhetoric than substance—denied the nation an opportunity even to order priorities and develop appropriate strategies to
meet postwar needs. Perhaps the closest the nation has come to
creating national objectives—a precursor, one would like to think, to
effective national human resource planning—was in establishing by
statute certain prescriptions concerning every American's right to
a decent home and job, those contained in the Housing Act of 1949 and
Employment Act of 1946. Unfortunately, however, neither act was
followed by a national commitment of resources sufficient to translate
laudable normative statements into reality.

Because state and city governments have been, in most instances,
unable—and in a few instances, unwilling—to assume essential welfare
and social service burdens, these functions have escalated to Washington. In essence, local governments have been left principally house-
keeping, public safety, and narrow environmental concerns. Their
capacity to meet human resource problems has been frustrated. Moreover, given their limited resources and, until recently, no articulate
local concern with the poor, their attempts to overcome their frustra-
tions has been nominal.

Federal programs, despite their number (more than 400), have
had only a marginal impact on human problems. This is so (1) because,
rhetoric to the contrary, this nation has never made a commitment of
resources sufficient to achieve measurable success and (2) because
the federal inventory, despite its coverage, presents users or potential
users with a complex, many times competitive, and sometimes dupli-
cating array of assistance options. These options often fail to respond
to the articulated needs and priorities of supposed beneficiaries.
Only rarely, and even then only with difficulty, can would-be sponsors,
including city halls, use more than one program at any one point in
time to initiate predefined strategies. In effect, coordinated use of
supposed complementary programs has been hard to achieve.

Unfortunately the War on Poverty was never really mounted,
partially because of a war in a far off country that was never
really terminated. OEO planners and funded local Community Action
Agencies granted primacy to defining "maximum feasible participation" at the expense of developing an operational definition of coordination at either the national or the local level. This "decision" led to
creation of countervailing resident-dominated structures in many
communities; the "opening up" of public decision-making processes

in some cities in a limited number of resource allocation areas; and
the initiation of marginally funded, though often innovative (always
numerous), projects in most cities. The War on Poverty, however,
unfortunately did not lead to more than cosmetic changes in the way
most public institutions delivered services in the majority of cities,
nor did it seriously engage the sustained attention and commitment
of more than a handful of local chief executives. Rarely were basic
city budgets affected. Given the very "public" distribution of limited
federal resources to the poor and the adversary strategy chosen by
OEO, the War on Poverty symbolized and perhaps at times unavoid-
ably heightened cleavages, particularly among poor blacks and blue
collar white ethnics.

Model Cities funds, unlike OEO monies, have flowed through
city hall. City Model Neighborhood Area resident group coalitions
have developed in many cities, and there seems to have been some
improvement in the capacity of some local institutions in many communities to meet objectives. Marginal White House commitment by
both the Johnson Administration and the Nixon Administration, however, combined with the difficulties inherent in the categorical program system, has impeded development of a suitable federal response
to developed city plans and programs. Early HUD planning guidelines,
since changed, relative to geographical imitations, "comprehensiveness," and "linkages," combined with pressures from neighborhoods,
and tight city budgets impeded strategic development of local priorities
concerning use of limited federal funds.

PROBLEMS AND CONSIDERATIONS

No longer does the nation have the "luxury" of "hidden" poverty.
No longer can we escape the fact that the difficulties facing those
who happen to be poor merely reflect the general malaise pervading
our institutions, our political processes, our people.

Poverty remains an inescapable fact of life for far too many
Americans. Efforts to eliminate or reduce it have been miniscule
compared to need and marginal with respect to results. Understandable contradictions exist side by side. Division, particularly between
black and white, less than affluent and not so affluent, chicano and
black, has accompanied the growing expectations and articulateness
of the poor. Similarly, alienation between the ghetto and city hall
has apparently continued in many communities despite modest signs
of change for the better in the role played by local institutions.

Racism—a euphemism for deep class and caste prejudices—
pervades many aspects of American life. It narrows choices open
to the affluent or near affluent as well as minority and lower income

households. It impedes development of necessary public and private services and limits the range of meaningful choices open to all Americans.

If we are to attempt seriously to meet the human needs of this nation, if we are to initiate the necessary actions to improve the quality of life of all Americans, we must be willing first to admit and then to resolve some basic problems.

1. Institutional Capacity, Money, and Decision Making: Many public institutions (federal, state and local) lack the capacity to manage even their currently identified functions, effectively much less accept new ones. Related to this problem is the fact that many state and local governments are caught in an ever worsening financial bind. For example, revenues in most cities appear to be rising at an annual rate of less than 5 percent while expenditures, most of them nondiscretionary, rise at rates approaching 10 percent.

2. Planners, Plans, and Decision Making: Planners and planning have made very little contribution toward either identifying or resolving human problems. The planner's quest for respectability has led him to substitute, more often than not, technique for insight; jargon for relevance; rhetoric for strategy. Terms and phrases like systems analyses, PPBS, goals, coordination, linkages, and priorities, despite the best of intentions, have not become operational in a decision-making context. They have meant little to federal officials faced with an annual appropriation cycle and a recalcitrant Congress; mayors whose resources are limited, whose agencies are hostile; residents of ghettos who are out of a job and whose children are hungry.

3. Politics and Decision Making Good intentions aside, it is unfortunately becoming increasingly difficult for national, state, and local leaders to articulate and then make tough decisions related to the collection and allocation of scarce resources. And the political risks involved in making such decisions are apparently vastly compounded if the beneficiaries of public action are clearly the poor, the black, or the chicano.

The national dialogue about priorities has become confused with such terms as forced integration. Governors willing to propose fiscal reform have run the risk of single terms in office; mayors appearing too sympathetic with objectives of minority constituencies often survive in office only by tight pluralities rather than majority votes. Indeed, most of the "good guys" face aborted careers as locally elected officials. Certainly, America's melting pot has cooled off (if it ever existed) and the benigness of its majority population more and more subject to debate.

Structural reform has been the long suit of critics of American institutions. Unfortunately, the reformers have rarely achieved a coincidence between their proposals and the real world. Today is no

different. Those who cry for decentralization and neighborhood government do their argument and their supposed constituency little good
when they neglect to weigh economic and indeed social benefits and
costs; when they refuse to become specific or selective concerning
functions, services, and processes; when they convert economic and
institutional facts of life to ideological demagoguery. Conversely,
those who argue for placing more responsibility for planning and
resource distribution in the hands of regional or state governments
(and subsequently taking responsibility from city governments and
the federal government) must come to reflect in their arguments
political, as well as institutional, realities. How many states are
equipped by inclination and capacity to accept more responsibility for
social planning and resource allocation? What about national performance criteria? Why is "areawide planning" any better than city or
neighborhood planning (for all functions and services; for some
functions and services)?

PROGRAMS: ALTERNATIVE APPROACHES

No easy solutions exist to the many and serious social problems
facing this nation. Unfortunately, however, we have accepted ground
rules defined by the academic egoist or the political jangoist in debating
federal policy issues and program approaches. For example, although
the Nixon Administration is to be congratulated for placing state
revenue sharing and family allowance plans before the Congress and
the country for discussion for the first time, neither proposal should
be viewed singly or together as presenting the possibility of achieving
"Nirvana". Both proposals must be complemented by others if they
themselves are to meet even limited Administration objectives. Each
proposal must be considered, and amended, in light of political,
institutional, and human problems.

State Revenue Sharing

Revenue sharing can be supported on any number of reasonable
grounds. It will, for example, provide states and local governments
with funds free of traditional categorical program restrictions.
Further, it will permit governments to secure such funds on a basis
free of pipeline considerations. As important, revenue sharing will
permit cities to justify more easily (politically) spending categorical
funds or funds like Model Cities in poverty areas. In effect, revenue
sharing may be the "bribe" necessary to permit mounting an effective
and meaningful War on Poverty for the first time.

Press stories relative to the Nixon Administration's revenue
sharing proposal indicate that the first year's share would be close
to $5 billion. At such a level, based on various formulas, only a
handful of cities would receive more than they do from current Model
Cities grants. Even if Model Cities and existing categorical programs
should continue to be funded at current levels, given state and city
needs, the adequacy of the reported revenue-sharing fund level is open
to question. Conversely, if other programs are cut back significantly, most cities will go beyond questioning and have problems
supporting the bill even as a beginning step.

Any revenue sharing proposal should (1) be based on income
and corporate tax yield; (2) have a pass-through formula reflecting
magnitude of local needs (particularly needs related to the poor); (3)
provide larger cities with a proportionately larger share of the total
proceeds; (4) be limited to general purpose governments; (5) contain
a post-audit for the purpose of reviewing expenditures in light of
national performance criteria (civil rights, for example); and (6)
provide incentives for superior performance in meeting national and
local performance pass-through.

Management/Planning

It is difficult to favor a continuation of most of 45 separately
funded federal planning programs. Of these, only the Model Cities
program has gone directly to and sometimes through the offices of
local chief executives. Moreover, only the Model Cities program and
a limited number of functionally oriented planning efforts have had
more than a ceremonial effect on most cities, particularly larger cities.
As implied earlier, despite contrary intentions, federal mandates
to be comprehensive and to define linkages combined with limitations
in funding have built a consulting industry rather than city capacity.
Such a history suggests choosing, instead, to provide state and local
governments with a simple open-ended management and priority
determination block grant, to go primarily to elected chief executives.
It could be used to develop a staff capacity to determine local problems
and to allocate and manage local resources effectively. Performance
criteria would pertain more to the role of the chief executive, agencies,
and appropriate resident groups than to the content or scope of any
plan. Such a grant would facilitate local government efforts relative
to the use of revenue sharing funds and categorical programs.

Categorical Programs

Categorical programs, despite the real problems mentioned above, have served to increase and improve the range and scope of a limited number of public services. They have also, given their number and varied routing systems as well as their performance criteria, guaranteed the poor at least a minimal amount of federal funds and services.

Institutional and political realities together with local needs provide sufficient support for continuation of the categorical program system—which does not mean, however, that the system should not be radically amended. AIP should support the following kinds of changes, particularly with regard to human community development and the concomitant allocation of resources.

1. Assuming development and inclusion of specific national performance criteria, including criteria requiring priority concern for the poor, the number of categorical programs (not the funding) should be vastly reduced and consolidated into functional block grants (social services, community development, and so forth).

2. Complementing such consolidation, statutory and administrative criteria should be amended to (a) extend the authorization and appropriation cycle; (b) eliminate all but functional earmarking with respect to administrative criteria; (c) direct funds to elected officials and general purpose governments; (d) provide for beneficiary involvement in planning and evaluating programs; (e) provide for post-audits rather than continuing program reviews by the sponsoring agency; (f) minimize processing events; and (g) facilitate joint agency funding.

Income Maintenance and Welfare

A basic component of any new legislative package should be an income maintenance program. President Nixon's family allowance plan provides a useful base upon which to build new legislation. It should not be reviewed by narrow partisan eyes. Given the nation's continued adherence (at least publically) to the Protestant ethic relative to work requirements, acceptance of the accompanying rhetoric could be an acceptable (necessary) price to pay for legislative enactment if onerous stipulations relative to these same requirements were actually eliminated or amended. A more important issue, the level of the allowance, should be debated vigorously. A minimum, approximately double the one proposed last year would be a proper point of departure. Similarly, federal assumption of all welfare costs should be considered by the Administration and Congress, if states and local governments divert money "saved" to national priority areas.

The four program thrusts mentioned above suggest at least an initial strategy to meet the nation's human problems. If they are accepted, the entire revenue and tax structure must be reexamined. No significant Vietnam peace dividend is apparently in prospect given the present state of the economy and ever increasing "nondiscretionary" needs. Certainly an evolving shift from local to federal collection of revenue is a proper subject for study, given the archaic and regressive nature of the local tax base. Similarly, continued elimination of corporate tax shelters and closing of loopholes would make the federal system more progressive and more lucrative.

As indicated in preceding chapters, a national dialogue concerning the role of the urban planner is needed. It should address several major facts of planning life in America today. This dialogue should be conducted in the context of an understanding that we do not yet have—

1. A full understanding of the impact of land use and land use arrangements on the lines of different types of people and groups.

2. A full understanding of the many and often complex linkages between and among the physical, social, and economic environments.

3. A full understanding of the means to predict or project with anything near certainty population and life styles.

4. A full understanding of the way to involve various kinds of individuals and groups meaningfully in the planning process.

Certainly, evidence suggests that the old adage that good neighborhoods make good people is much too simplistic a principle upon which to premise the allocation of increasingly scarce urban resources. Indeed, if choices relative to dollar expenditures must be made and if our objective is to seek a better life for the poor, priority attention should be granted to social and economic goods and services rather than to physical considerations.

Partly because of the marginal state of the planner's knowledge and partly because of the many isms governing his behavior, he has, as outlined in this text, concentrated much of his activity (or at least his rhetoric) in the long range, comprehensive planning area. He has thus generally been able to substitute art for methodology and whim for technique. Unfortunately, his limitations have made his efforts almost irrelevant to current public decision-making processes concerning urban policy and programs—policies and programs that, for the first time, are being forced to reflect serious caste/class and life style differences in the nation's make-up.

To become an effective participant in a hoped-for decade-long, major national effort to resolve urban ills, the planner will have to reevaluate and amend his approaches. He will have to—

1. Mute a desire for comprehensive, long range vision in order to make selected efforts at problem solving in restricted, well-defined geographic areas.

2. Substitute an increasing ability to provide immediate answers for the ephemeral endeavor to be a soothsayer for future problems and future populations.

3. Replace an outmoded corporate or utilitarian view of urban life with a better understanding of the many and diverse game players now competing for scarce urban resources.

4. Accept the fact that certainty is rare with respect to most proposed solutions to urban problems and the fact that "the public interest" is in many cases a convenient ruse for legitimizing the interests of some particular elements of the urban populations.

Clearly it has been argued in this volume that urban planning must be viewed in terms of resource allocation. And in these terms politics is the sine qua non planning. Involvement of residents and elected officials in the planning process is necessary not only to help the planner define problems, goals, and solutions but also to help him set priorities. In the process the planner should not fear to make his own value system a known and an acknowledged factor in the planning process—and it is to be hoped that it will reflect a basic humanism rather than an abstract ideology. It is also to be hoped that it will grant the poor priority attention.

MARSHALL KAPLAN is Principal in the firm of Marshall Kaplan, Gans, and Kahn in San Francisco. Mr. Kaplan has directed for his firm the national HUD-funded study of the Model Cities program; the U.S. Senate's analyses of CAAs in the Western Region; and the HUD-sponsored Urban Technical Services Pool. He has served as an advisor to many presidential task forces and commissions on urban problems; was a consultant to Robert Kennedy's Bedford-Stuyvesant program; has served as a consultant to the Land Use Subcommittee of the Academy of Sciences; and is now a member of the Academy's Subcommittee on Planning Programs. He is also serving as an advisor to several New Town developers, and recently chaired the HUD Task Force on Simplification and Consolidation.

Mr. Kaplan has taught at several universities, and has authored many books and articles on New Towns, urban problems, and the role of the planner.

Mr. Kaplan has an M.A. in City Planning from MIT; an M.A. in Public Administration from Boston University; and a B.A. in Political Science from Boston University.

www.ingramcontent.com/pod-product-compliance
Lightning Source LLC
Chambersburg PA
CBHW020356270326
41926CB00007B/461